Biography

James Egan was born in 1985 and grew up in Portarlington, Co. Laois in the Midlands of Ireland.
In 2008, James moved to England and studied in Oxford. James married his wife in 2012 and currently lives in Havant in Hampshire.
James had his first book, 365 Ways to Stop Sabotaging Your Life, published in 2014.
Several of James' books have become No.1 Best Sellers in the UK including 1000 Facts about Horror Movies, 3000 Facts About the Greatest Movies Ever, 365 Things People Believe That Aren't True, Another 365 Things People Believe That Aren't True, and 500 Things People Believe That Aren't True.

3,000 Astounding Quotes

By

James Egan

ISBN: 9781326400378

Lulu Publishing Services rev. date: 24/08/2015

Dedicated to John, my mentor who, after all of these years, never stops teaching me

1. We must overact our part in some measure, in order to produce any effect at all.

    \- William Hazlitt

2. A man once told Buddha, "I want happiness."
   Buddha replied, "First, remove "I"; that's ego.
   Then remove 'want'; that's desire.
   And now all you're left with is happiness.

    \- Budai

3. We encounter the call unanswered; for it is possible to turn the ear to other interests.

    \- Anon

4. We can either hang together or hang separately.

    \- Benjamin Franklin

5. Wise men don't need advice. Fools won't take it.

    \- Benjamin Franklin

6. Better never to have met you in my dream than to wake and reach for hands that are not there.

    \- Otomo No Yakamochi

7. The only thing to do with good advice is to pass it on. It is never of any use to oneself.

    \- Anon

8. Water is formless and flows. But if you put it in a cup, its shape becomes the cup. If you put it in a teapot, it becomes the teapot. Be like water.

    \- Bruce Lee

9. Adapt yourself to the things among which your lot has been cast and love sincerely the fellow creatures with whom destiny has ordained you shall live.

    \- Marcus Aurelius

10. It is not good enough to have a good man. The main thing is to use it well.

    \- Rene Descartes

11. Your net worth to the world is usually determined by what remains after your bad habits are subtracted from your good ones.

- Benjamin Franklin

12. I admire anyone who rids himself of an addiction.

- Gene Tierney

13. Every form of addiction is bad, whether it be alcohol or morphine or idealism.

- Carl Jung

14. It is better to be seventy years young than forty years old.

- Oliver Wendell Holmes Jr.

15. My words fly up, my thoughts remain below; Words without thoughts never to heaven go.

- William Shakespeare

16. We are what we repeatedly do. Excellence, therefore, is not an act, but a habit.

- Aristotle

17. A comfortable old age is the reward of a well-spent youth.

- Maurice Chevalier

18. We feel instinctively that the good is something proper to its possessor and not easily taken from him.

- Aristotle

19. Alone we can do little; together we can do so much.

- Helen Keller

20. A man cannot be comfortable without his own approval.

- Anon

21. If we have no peace, it is because we have forgotten that we belong to each other.

- Mother Teresa

22. It is the mark of an educated man to look for precision in each class of thing in so far as its nature admits.

- Aristotle

23. We desire something because we believe it to be good than that we believe a thing to be good because we desire it.

- Aristotle

24. You can't fill a cup that's already full.

- Anon

25. You cannot shake hands with a clenched fist.

- Mahatma Gandhi

26. Everybody has a secret world inside of them. I mean everybody. All of the people in the whole world – no matter how dull and boring they are on the outside. Inside them they've all got unimaginable, magnificent, wonderful, stupid, amazing worlds… Not just one world. Hundreds of them. Thousands, maybe.

- Neil Gaiman

27. Appreciation is wonderful: It makes what is excellent in others belong to us.

- Voltaire

28. Too much agreement kills a chat.

- Eldridge Cleaver

29. With confidence, you have won before you have started.

- Marcus Garvey

30. Believe those who are seeking the truth. Doubt those who find it.

- Andre Gide

31. When I was a child, my mother said to me, "If you become a soldier, you'll be a general. If you become a monk, you'll end up as the pope. Instead, I became a painter and wound up as Picasso.

- Pablo Picasso

32. Since reality is incomplete, art must not be too much afraid of incompleteness.

- Iris Murdoch

33. If you would not be forgotten, as soon as you are dead and rotten, either write things worth reading, or do things worth the writing.

- Benjamin Franklin

34. Any man who reads too much and uses his own brain too little falls into lazy habits of thinking.

- Albert Einstein

35. You may delay but time will not.

- Benjamin Franklin

36. Imagination is a quality given a man to compensate him for what he is not, and a sense of humor was provided to console him for what he is.

- Oscar Wilde

37. God helps them that helps themselves.

- Benjamin Franklin

38. We all know that Art is not truth. Art is a lie that makes us realize truth.

- Pablo Picasso

39. Never leave that till tomorrow which you can do today.

- Benjamin Franklin

40. If you're riding ahead of the herd, take a look back every now and then to make sure it's still there.

- Will Rogers

41. I am patient with stupidity but not with those who are proud of it.

- Edith Sitwell

42. Always bear in mind that your own resolution to succeed, is more important than any other one thing.

- Abraham Lincoln

43. Don't fear failure. Not failure, but low aim, is the crime. In great attempts it is glorious even to fail.

- Bruce Lee

44. Real friendship is shown in times of trouble.

- Anon

45. The believer is happy, the doubter is wise.

- Hungarian Proverb

46. To be prepared for war is one of the most effective means of preserving peace.

- George Washington

47. Everything was once impossible until someone did it.

- Anon

48. Association with human beings lures one into self-observation.

- Franz Kafka

49. Just be who you want to be, not what others want to see.

- Anon

50. Not even the sun shines at all times throughout the day.

- Anon

51. Nothing is impossible. Even the word itself says, "I'm possible."

- Audrey Hepburn

52. There are no gains without pains.

- Benjamin Franklin

53. My attitude is that if you push me towards something that you think is a weakness, then I will turn that perceived weakness into a strength.

- Michael Jordan

54. Attitude is a little thing that makes a big difference.

- Winston Churchill

55. A life is like a garden. Perfect moments can be had, but not preserved, except in memory. Live long and prosper.

- Leonard Nimoy

56. A man only learns in two ways, one by reading, and the other by association with smarter people.

- Will Rogers

57. Children are the world's most valuable resource and its best hope for the future.

- John F. Kennedy

58. You can get everything in life you want if you will just help enough other people get what they want.

- Zig Ziglar

59. Nothing is really work unless you would rather be doing something else.

- J.M. Barrie

60. I suspect the secret of personal attraction is locked up in our unique imperfections, flaws and frailties.

- Hugh Mackay

61. Human progress is neither automatic nor inevitable... Every step toward the goal of justice requires sacrifice.

- Martin Luther King, Jr.

62. A truly strong person does not need the approval of others any more than a lion needs the approval of sheep.

- Vernon Howard

63. A doubtful friend is worse than a certain enemy.

- Aesop

64. Some people act without thinking. What's even worse is thinking without acting.

- Anon

65. Success is never final. Failure is never fatal. It is courage that counts.

- Winston Churchill

66. One child, one teacher, one book and one pen can change the world.

- Malala Yousafzai

67. Most of us attract by default. We just think we don't have any control over it. Our feelings are on autopilot and so everything is brought to us by default.

- Bob Doyle

68. Respect people who find time for you in their busy schedule. But love people who never look at their schedule when you need them.

- Anon

69. Please all and you will please none.

- Aesop

70. Kids – in a really good way – can talk about their differences without the baggage that adults have.

- Jim McKay

71. If you're interested in "balancing" work and pleasure, stop trying to balance them. Instead make your work more pleasurable.

- Anon

72. The truth is like a lion. You don't have to defend it. Let it loose. It will defend itself.

- Anon

73. To err is human, to forgive is divine.

- Alexander Pope

74. A peacock taunted a crane with the dullness of her plumage. "Look at my brilliant colors" cackled the peacock.
Replied the crane, "But when it comes to flying, I can soar whereas you are confined to the earth."

- Aesop

75. The most blind is not the ones who can't see but the ones who choose not to.

- Anon

76. I don't share my thoughts because I think it will change the minds of people who think differently. I share my thought to show the people who already think like me that they're not alone.

- Anon

77. A man can fail many times but he is not a failure until he blames somebody else.

- John Burroughs

78. The most complex object in the known universe, the brain, only uses 20 watts of power. It would require a nuclear power plant to energize a computer the size of a city block to mimic your brain, and your brain does it with just 20 watts. So if someone calls you dim bulb, that's a compliment.

- Michio Kaku

79. Be a loner. That gives you time to wonder, to search for the truth. Have holy curiosity. Make your life worth living.

- Albert Einstein

80. Bitter experience has taught us how fundamental our values are and how great the mission they represent.

- Jan Peter Balkenende

81. Spend life with who makes you happy, not who you have to impress.

- Anon

82. Subdue your appetites, my dears, and you've conquered human nature.

- Charles Dickens

83. One man's blasphemy doesn't override other people's free-speech rights, their freedom to publish, freedom of thought.

- Dan Savage

84. Almost every wise saying has an opposite one, no less wise, to balance it.

- George Santayana

85. The most dangerous phrase is, "We've always done it this way."

- Anon

86. I believe that a simple and unassuming manner of life best for everyone, best both for the body and the mind.

- Albert Einstein

87. It is no use saying, "We are doing our best." You have got to succeed in doing what is necessary.

- Winston Churchill

88. If you only read the books that everyone is reading, you can only think what everyone else is thinking.

- H.P. Lovecraft

89. The pen is mightier than the sword.

- Edward Bulwer-Lytton

90. The greatest lesson in life is to know that even fools are right sometimes.

- Winston Churchill

91. In heaven, all the interesting people are missing.

- Friedrich Nietzsche

92. Ambition leads me not only farther than any other has been before me, but as far as I think it possible for man to go.

- James Cook

93. Work hard in silence. Let success makes the noise.

- Anon

94. Nothing in life is to be feared, it is only to be understood.

- Marie Curie

95. Everyone you will ever meet knows something you don't.

- Bill Nye

96. It is not by muscle, speed or physical dexterity that great things are achieved, but by reflection, force of character, and judgment.

- Marcus Tullius Cicero

97. Accuracy of observation is the equivalent of accuracy of thinking.

- Wallace Stevens

98. Forgive your enemies, but never forget their names.

- John F. Kennedy

99. If you make listening and observation your occupation you will gain much more than you can by talk.

- Robert Baden-Powell

100. The greatest enemy of knowledge is not ignorance, it is the illusion of knowledge.

- Stephen Hawking

101. Simply by sailing in a new direction you could enlarge the world.

- Allen Curnow
(Landfall in Unknown Seas)

102. Never be ashamed of a scar. It simply means you were stronger than whatever tried to hurt you.

- Anon

103. A man has always to be busy with his thoughts if anything is to be accomplished.

- Antonie van Leeuwenhoek

104. To change the world, you have to change yourself.

- Anon

105. Scars remind us that past is real.

- Thomas Harris

106. Don't play with fire but get close enough to stay warm.

- Anon

107. Weak people revenge. Strong people forgive. Intelligent people ignore.

- Albert Einstein

108. Because things are the way they are, they will not stay the way they are.

- Bertolt Brecht

109. Life is not measured by the number of breaths we take, but by the moments that take our breath away.

- Maya Angelou

110. The source of one of our biggest complaints is our inability to adjust to change.

- Anon

111. I was not born for one corner, the whole world is my native land.

- Anon

112. The injuries we do and those we suffer are seldom weighed in the same scales.

- Aesop

113. After all is said and done, more is said than done.

- Aesop

114.   He that always gives way to others will end in having no principles of his own.

- Aesop

115.   Whatever you are, be a good one.

- Abraham Lincoln

116.   A crust eaten in peace is better than a banquet partaken in anxiety.

- Anon

117.   People are so obstinate; they actually refuse to change, not realizing that it's not viable in an ever-changing world.

- Anon

118.   A lot of people don't fix their problems, and they don't stop sabotaging themselves because they're use to it, and the alternative requires effort.

- Anon

119.   Our insignificance is often the cause of our safety.

- Aesop

120.   I'm a slow walker, but I never walk back.

- Abraham Lincoln

121.   No man has a good enough memory to be a successful liar.

- Abraham Lincoln

122.   Those who deny freedom to others deserve it not for themselves; and under the rule of a just God, cannot long retain it.

- Abraham Lincoln

123.   We must do away with the absolutely specious notion that everybody has to earn a living. It is a fact today that one in ten thousand of us can make a technological breakthrough capable of supporting all the rest. The youth of today are absolutely right in recognizing this nonsense of earning a living. We keep inventing jobs because of this false idea that everybody has to be employed at some kind of drudgery because, according to Malthusian-Darwinian theory, he must justify his rights to exist. So we have inspectors of inspectors and people making instruments for inspectors to inspect

inspectors. The true business of people should be to go back to school and think about whatever it was they were thinking about before somebody came along and told them they had to earn a living.

— Richard Buckminster Fuller

124.   The only source of knowledge is experience.

— Albert Einstein

125.   All progress has resulted from people taking unwanted positions in life throughout history.

— Anon

126.   Once you say you're going to settle for a second, that's what happens to you in life, I find.

— John F. Kennedy

127.   Be kind for everyone you meet is fighting a hard battle.

— Anon

128.   Do not pray for an easy life, pray for the strength to endure a difficult one.

— Bruce Lee

129.   Keep away from people who try to belittle your ambitions. Small people always do that, but the really great make you feel that you, too, can become great.

— Mark Twain

130.   The time to repair the roof is when the sun is shining.

— John F. Kennedy

131.   Live for nothing or die for something.

— Sylvester Stallone

132.   Never interrupt your enemy when he is making a mistake.

— Napoleon Bonaparte

133.   I am not bound to win, but I am bound to be true. I am not bound to succeed, but I am bound to live by the light that I have. I must stand with anybody that stands right, and stand with him while he is right, and part with him when he goes wrong.

— Abraham Lincoln

134. Oh, East is East, and West is West, and never the twain shall meet, Till Earth and Sky stand presently at Gods great Judgment Seat; But there is neither East nor West, Border, nor Breed, nor Birth, When two strong men stand face to face, tho they come from the ends of the earth.

- Rudyard Kipling

135. I think and think for months and years. Ninety-nine times, the conclusion is false. The hundredth time I am right.

- Albert Einstein

136. Advice is what we ask for when we already know the answer but wish we didn't.

- Erica Mann Jong

137. There was never a good war or a bad peace.

- Benjamin Franklin

138. If you change, remember: don't change back. Just because something has changed doesn't mean it can't change again. Change is the only constant in life.

- Anon

139. When you come to the end of your rope, tie a knot and hang on.
- Franklin D. Roosevelt

140. It's not about how hard you hit. It's about how hard you get hit and you keep getting back up.

- Sylvester Stallone

141. Nobody likes change, but it's the only thing that brings progress.
- Anon

142. You cannot help men permanently by doing for them what they could and should do for themselves.

- William Boetcker

143. God, grant me the serenity to accept the things I cannot change, courage to change the things I can, and the wisdom to know the difference.

- Reinhold Niebuhr

144. People look at their state of affairs and say "This is who I am." That's not who you are. That's who you were. If you don't have enough money in your bank account, that's not who you are, that's the residual outcome of your past thoughts and actions. If you define yourself into your current affairs, you doom yourself to nothing more but the same in the future.

- James Ray

145. Being honest may not get you many friends but it'll always get you the right ones.

- John Lennon

146. An era can be said to end when its basic illusions are exhausted.

- Arthur Miller

147. We keep talking of the world of tomorrow, doing little to change the world that is.

- Anon

148. Nobody can make a greater mistake than those who do nothing because they could only do a little.

- Aristotle

149. Progress as if success is inevitable.

- Anon

150. We have it in our power to begin the world again.

- Thomas Paine

151. It's not about charisma and personality, it's about results.

- Steve Jobs

152. Your beliefs don't make you a better person. Your behavior does.

- Anon

153. Do the best you can until you know better. Then when you know better, do better.

- Maya Angelou

154. If one doesn't know what they want, any opportunity is the right opportunity.

- Anon

155.   Today you are you, and that is truer than true. There is no one alive who is youer than you.

- Dr. Seuss

156.   Every choice you make has an end result.

- Zig Ziglar

157.   Do not brood over your past mistakes and failures as this will only fill your mind with grief, regret and depression. Do not repeat them in the future.

- Sivananda

158.   What an astonishing thing a book is. It's a flat object made from a tree with flexible parts on which are imprinted lots of funny dark squiggles. But one glance at it and you're inside the mind of another person, maybe somebody dead for thousands of years across the millennia, an author is speaking clearly and silently inside your head, directly to you. Writing is perhaps the greatest of human inventions, bind together people who never knew each other, citizens of distant epochs. Books break the shackles of time. A book is proof that humans are capable of working magic.

- Carl Sagan

159.   Believe you are defeated, believe it long enough and it is likely to become a fact.

- Norman Vincent Peale

160.   A mind always employed is always happy. This is the true secret, the grand recipe.

- Thomas Jefferson

161.   The best executive is one who has sense enough to pick good people to do what he wants done, and self-restraint enough to keep from meddling with them while they do it.

- Theodore Roosevelt

162.   I think the saddest people always try their hardest to make people happy. Because they know what it's like to feel absolutely worthless and they don't want anybody else to feel like that.

- Robin Williams

163.   Begin thus from the first act, and proceed; and, in conclusion, at the ill which thou hast done, be troubled, and rejoice for the good.

- Pythagoras

164.   The highest form of ignorance is when you reject something you don't know anything about.

- Wayne Dyer

165.   Don't settle with someone you can live with. Settle with someone you can't live without.

- Anon

166.   Being single means you're strong enough to wait for what you deserve.

- Anon

167.   Common sense is the most fairly distributed thing in the world, for each one thinks he is so well-endowed with it that even those who are hardest to satisfy in all other matters are not in the habit of desiring more of it than they already have.

- Rene Descartes

168.   Whether you think you can or think you can't, either way, you're right.

- Henry Ford

169.   I hate complacency. I play every gig as if it could be my last, then I enjoy it more.

- Nigel Kennedy

170.   We are the granddaughters of the witches you weren't able to burn.

- Anon

171.   Men are much better than their ordinary life allows them to be.
- J. B. Priestley

172.   The good thing about science is that it's true whether or not you believe in it.

- Neil de Grasse Tyson.

173.   99% of who we are is invisible and untouchable.
- R. Buckminster Fuller

174. We can tune into frequencies and see pictures on our tv. We choose what to see and hear by changing the channel and switching the frequency. We can apply the same way of thinking to life.

- Dr. Joe Vitale

175. What if the cure for cancer is trapped inside the mind of someone who can't afford an education?

- Anon

176. A positive attitude causes a chain reaction of positive thoughts, events and outcomes. It is a catalyst and it sparks extraordinary results.

- Wade Boggs

177. The same boiling water that softens the potato hardens the egg. It's not about the circumstances, but rather what you are made of.

- Anon

178. No phenomenon can be isolated, but has repercussions through all of our lives.

- Arthur Erickson

179. If you're giving your all and it's not enough, you're probably giving it to the wrong person.

- Anon

180. There's nothing so bad that it couldn't be worse.

- Irish Proverb

181. Knowledge is having the right answer.
Intelligence is asking the right question.

- Anon

182. Better the rudest work that tells a story, than the richest without meaning.

- John Ruskin

183. The philosophy of the school room in one generation will be the philosophy of government in the next.

- Abraham Lincoln

184.   The probability that we may fail in the struggle ought not to deter us from the support of a cause we believe to be just.

- Abraham Lincoln

185.   Once we accept our limits, we go beyond them.

- Albert Einstein

186.   Having been an educator for so many years I know that all a good teacher can do is set a context and raise questions.

- Godfrey Reggio

187.   Educating yourself doesn't mean that you were stupid in the first place; it means that you are intelligent enough to know that there is plenty to learn.

- Melanie Joy

188.   If people keep throwing stuff at you, build something with it.

- Anon

189.   The genie is a metaphor that you have the power to wish anything into being because you believe you can. The universe is at your command.

- James Ray

190.   Every exit is an entrance to a different place.

- Anon

191.   There is no cure for birth and death save to enjoy the interval.

- George Santayana

192.   Maybe this world is another planet's hell.

- Aldous Huxley

193.   Better be wise by the misfortunes of others than by your own.

- Aesop

194.   No matter how slow you're running, you're still lapping everyone who's at home sitting on the sofa.

- Anon

195.   It takes as much energy to wish as it does to plan.

- Eleanor Roosevelt

196. Never ascribe to malice that which can adequately be explained by incompetence.

- Napoleon Bonaparte

197. The way to see by Faith is to shut the Eye of Reason.

- Benjamin Franklin

198. One thing about growing up is realizing you don't hate anything anymore. Things either matter to you or they don't.

- Anon

199. Imagination is the preview for life's coming attractions.

- Albert Einstein

200. No great improvements in the lot of mankind are possible, until a great change takes place in the fundamental constitution of their modes of thought.

- John Stuart Mill

201. Whenever you are to do a thing, though it can never be known but to yourself, ask yourself how you would act were all the world looking at you, and act accordingly.

- Thomas Jefferson

202. The language of friendship is not words, but meanings.

- Henry David Thoreau

203. They laugh at me because I'm different; I laugh at them because they're all the same.

- Anon

204. If you would be loved, love and be loveable.

- Benjamin Franklin

205. All human beings should try to learn before they die what they are running from and to and why.

- James Thurber

206. Whatever the mind can conceive and believe, the mind can achieve.

- Napoleon Hill

207. If we wait until we are ready, we will be waiting for the rest of our lives.

- Lemony Snicket

208. You cannot escape the responsibility of tomorrow by evading it today.

- Abraham Lincoln

209. If your dreams don't scare you, they are too small.

- Richard Branson

210. You think you can just skim over the surface, barely ever making contact. Then you realize that where you're running is nowhere, and everything you want is under the surface. It'll hurt digging through it, but it will be worth it.

- Anon

211. The things I want to know are in books; my best friend is the man who'll get me a book I ain't read.

- Abraham Lincoln

212. An old Cherokee told his grandson, "There is a battle between two wolves inside us all. One is Evil. It is anger, jealousy, greed, resentment, inferiority, lies, and ego. The other is Good. It is joy, peace, love, hope, humility, kindness, empathy, and truth." The boy thought about it and asked, "Grandfather, which wolf wins?"
The old man quietly replied, "The one you feed."

- Anon

213. A good teacher must know the rules; a good pupil, the exceptions.

- Martin H. Fischer

214. Why accept the second rate version of yourself?

- David Mamet

215. An expert is someone who knows some of the worst mistakes that can be made in his subject and who manages to avoid them.

- Werner Heisenberg

216. I have not failed; I have just found 10,000 ways that don't work.

- Thomas Edison

217. Beware lest you lose the substance by grasping the shadow.

- Aesop

218. Whoever is careless with the truth in small matters cannot be trusted with important matters.

- Albert Einstein

219. I have found that, to make a contented slave, it is necessary to make a thoughtless one. It is necessary to darken his moral and mental vision as far as possible, to annihilate the power of reason. He must be able to detect no inconsistencies. He must be made to feel that slavery is right and he can be brought to that only when he ceased to be a man.

- Frederick Douglass

220. If you don't quit, you can't fail.

- Anon

221. Everybody is a genius. But if you judge a fish by its ability to climb a tree, it will live its whole life believing that it is stupid.

- Albert Einstein

222. Don't worry when you are not recognized, but strive to be worthy of recognition.

- Abraham Lincoln

223. A failure can help you succeed more than a success.

- Anon

224. You have enemies? Good. That means you've stood up to something, sometime in your life.

- Winston Churchill

225. You need to learn to fall to learn to stand.

- Anon

226. Studios are okay with a movie failing the same way over and over. What's wrong with failing a new way? You haven't tried it before so at least failing isn't a guarantee!

- Steven Soderbergh

227. How you deal with your failure is more important than the
failure itself.

- Anon

228. What if I fall?
Oh, but darling, what if you fly?

- Esther Harrison

229. Good people fail every day. Great people keep going until they
succeed.

- Anon

230. She walks in Beauty, like the night
Of cloudless climes and starry skies
And all that's best of dark and bright
Meet in her aspect and her eyes:
Thus mellow'd to that tender light
Which heaven to gaudy day denies.

- Lord Byron

231. When you talk, you are only repeating what you already know.
But if you listen, you may learn something new.

- Dalai Lama

232. Character is like a tree and reputation like a shadow. The
shadow is what we think of it; the tree is the real thing.

- Abraham Lincoln

233. A picture is worth a thousand words.

- Fred R. Bernard

234. You are only as good as your losses.

- Anon

235. Buddha was asked, "What have you gained from meditation?"
He replied, "Nothing! However, let me tell you what I have lost:
anger, anxiety, depression, insecurity, fear of old age and death.

- Budai

236. Don't see where you have failed but where you have succeeded.

- Anon

237. The miracle is this; the more we share, the more we have.

- Leonard Nimoy

238. We have not failed until we have exhausted every possibility.

- Albert Einstein

239. The greatest achievers in the world have their accomplishments built on a mountain of failure.

- Anon

240. We met for a reason, either you're a blessing or a lesson.

- Anon

241. Obstacles are those frightful things you see when you take your eyes off the goal.

- Henry Ford

242. I can't tell you the key to success, but the key to failure is trying to please everyone.

- Ed Sheeran

243. Getting rid of a delusion makes us wiser than getting hold of a truth.

- Ludwig Borne

244. Favors too plentiful will be lost, favors far and between will always be remembered and treasured.

- Anon

245. The chief danger in life is that you take too many precautions.

- Alfred Adler

246. Courage is not the absence of fear but the capacity for action despite our fears.

- Mark Twain

247. Everybody has their day and some days last longer than others.

- Winston Churchill

248. For me, it is far better to grasp the Universe as it really is than to persist in delusion, however satisfying and reassuring.

- Carl Sagan

249. Discussion is just a tool. You have to aim; the final goal must be a decision.

- Harri Holkeri

250. Coming together is a beginning; keeping together is progress; working together is success.

- Henry Ford

251. All creatures are flawed, but out of the flaw may come the universe.

- Marguerite Young

252. No man is wise at all times.

- Pliny the Elder

253. Choosing not to forgive is choosing to stay angry.

- Mike Fisher

254. We read that we ought to forgive our enemies; but we do not read that we ought to forgive our friends.

- Cosimo de' medici

255. A friend is a single soul dwelling in twin bodies.

- Aristotle

256. The only way to have a friend is to be one

- Ralph Waldo Emerson.

257. We have fewer friends than we imagine, but more than we know.

- Hugo von Hofmannsthal

258. Twenty years from now, you will be more disappointed by the things that you didn't do than by the ones you did do, so throw off the bowlines, sail away from safe harbor, catch the trade winds in your sails. Explore. Dream. Discover.

- Mark Twain

259. There is always one moment in childhood when the door opens and lets the future in.

- Graham Greene

260. I'm not interested in competing with anyone. I hope we all make it.

- Erica Cook

261. Every strike brings me closer to the next home run.

- Babe Ruth

262. I attribute my success to this: I never gave or took any excuse.

- Florence Nightingale

263. Do not fear the future. If you knew your future, it would hold no surprises, wonder, or suspense. It would shackle you to permanent triviality. It would trap you in a past that hasn't happened yet. It makes you a prisoner of your fate and a slave to your destiny.

- Anon

264. If it can be destroyed by the truth, it deserves to be destroyed by the truth.

- Carl Sagan

265. Definiteness of purpose is the starting point of all achievement.

- W. Clement Stone

266. Everyone's a part of what happens next.

- Anon

267. You cannot escape the responsibility of tomorrow by evading it today.

- Abraham Lincoln

268. If you can't fly, then run.
If you can't run, then walk.
If you can't walk, then crawl.
But whatever you do, you have to keep moving.

- Martin Luther King

269. I am not sure what the future will bring, but I accept the future will come. I will rise to meet it.

- Anon

270. The best way to predict the future is to invent it.

- Anon

271.   Strive not to be a success, but rather to be of value.

          - Albert Einstein

272.   Life isn't about getting and having, it's about giving and being.

          - Kevin Kruse

273.   Life is 10% what happens to me and 90% of how I react to it.

          - Charles Swindoll

274.   We become what we think about.

          - Earl Nightingale

275.   I've missed more than 9000 shots in my career. I've lost almost
300 games. 26 times, I've been trusted to take the game winning
shot and missed. I've failed over and over and over again in my life.
And that is why I succeed.

          - Michael Jordan

276.   Do not worry about tomorrow for tomorrow will worry about
itself. Each day has enough trouble on its own.

          - St. James Bible

277.   Giving's better than lending and costs around the same.

          - Anon

278.   The most common way people give up their power is by
thinking they don't have any.

          - Alice Walker

279.   The mind is everything. What you think becomes.

          - Buddha

280.   The best time to plant a tree was 20 years ago. The second-best
time is now.

          - Chinese Proverb

281.   We have no more right to consume happiness without producing
it than to consume wealth without producing it.

          - George Bernard Shaw

282.   All that we are is a result of what we thought.

          - Buddha

283. They ignore you now, but they'll need you later.

- Anon

284. I am looking for a lot of men who have infinite capacity to not know what can be done.

- Henry Ford

285. Pleasure in the job puts perfection in the work.

- Aristotle

286. You have never lived until you have done something for someone who can't repay you.

- Anon

287. Follow your bliss and the universe will open doors for you where there were only walls.

- Joseph Campbell

288. An unexamined life is not worth living.

- Socrates

289. Leave nothing but footprints. Take nothing but pictures. Kill nothing but time.

- Anon

290. Don't work harder, work smarter.

- Steve Woodward

291. Be with someone who would drive five hours just to see you for one.

- Anon

292. Darkness cannot drive out darkness; only light can do that. Hate cannot drive out hate; only love can do that.

- Martin Luther King

293. Every generalization is dangerous. Even this one.

- Alexandre Dumas

294. Your time is limited, so don't waste it living someone else's life.

- Steve Jobs

295. At the age of six I wanted to be a cook. At seven I wanted to be Napoleon. And my ambition has been growing steadily ever since.

- Salvador Dali

296. Eighty percent of success is showing up.

- Woody Allen

297. Whoever is careless with the truth in small matters cannot be trusted with important matters.

- Albert Einstein

298. Think of a car driving through the night. The headlights only go two hundred feet forward, and you can make it all the way to New York driving through the dark because all you have to see is the next two hundred feet. And that's how life tends to unfold before us. If we just trust the next two hundred feet, and we know that the next two hundred feet will follow after that, life will keep unfolding. And it will eventually get you to your destination or whatever it is you truly want because you want it.

- Jack Canfield

299. I am not a product of my circumstances. I am a product of my decisions.

- Stephen Covey

300. If you love a flower, don't pick it up. Because if you pick it up, it dies and it ceases to be what you love. So if you love a flower, let it be. Love is not about possession. Love is about appreciation.

- Osho

301. Winning isn't everything, wanting to win is.

- Vince Lombardi

302. We cling to our own ideals and hope in the face of adversary, we will be strong enough to stand by them.

- Anon

303. Be kind to everything that lives.

- Anon

304. He has a right to criticize, who has a heart to help.

- Abraham Lincoln

305. To take away a mountain, move it stone by stone.

- Anon

306. Look at life as a tree. You can be a leaf that falls off, a twig that holds the leaf, a branch that protects many leaves, the roots that keep everything up, or the trunk that makes the body.
All of the parts of a tree rely on another part of a tree to survive, no matter how small those parts are or how small their job seems.

- Anon

307. We cannot teach people anything; we can only help them discover it within themselves.

- Galileo Galilei

308. We are not makers of history. We are made by history.

- Martin Luther King, Jr.

309. Maybe if we look hard enough, we can stop making the same mistakes and continue making the same advancements.

- Anon

310. Humor is the weapon of unarmed people: it helps people who are oppressed to smile at the situation that pains them.

- Simon Wiesenthal

311. Men travel faster now, but I do not know if they go to better things.

- Willa Cather
(Death Comes for the Archbishop)

312. Don't tell me the sky's the limit when there are footprints on the Moon.

- Melody Hossaini

313. Once an idea has taken hold of the brain it's almost impossible to eradicate. An idea that is fully formed - fully understood - that sticks; right in there somewhere.

- Domm Cobb
(Inception)

314. Isn't just the existence of life significant?

- Alan Moore

315. "I'm bored" is a useless thing to say. You live in a great, big vast world that you've seen none percent of. And even the inside of your own mind is endless. It goes on forever inwardly. Do you understand? Being the fact that you're alive is amazing, so you don't get to be bored.

- Louie C.K.

316. The salvation of mankind lies only in making everything the concern of all.

- Alexander Solzehnitsyn

317. The first step in a person's salvation is knowledge of their sin.

- Lucius Annaeus Seneca

318. The chessboard is the world; the pieces are the phenomena of the universe. The rules of the game are what we call the laws of Nature. The player on the other side is hidden from us. We know that his play is always fair, just, and patient. But also we know, to our cost, that he never overlooks a mistake, or makes the smallest allowance for ignorance.

- T.H. Huxley

319. Love comes when manipulation stops; when you think more about the other person than about his or her reactions to you. When you dare to reveal yourself fully. When you dare to be vulnerable.

- The Joyce Brothers

320. Consciousness is the phenomenon whereby the universe's very existence is made known.

- Roger Penrose

321. Take the first step in fate. You don't have to see the whole staircase. Just take the first step.

- Martin Luther King Jr.

322. This is a story about four people named Everybody, Somebody, Anybody and Nobody.There was an important job to be done and Everybody was sure that Somebody would do it.
Anybody could have done it, but Nobody did it. Somebody got angry about that, because it was Everybody's job. Everybody thought Anybody could do it, but Nobody realized that Everybody wouldn't do it.

It ended up that Everybody blamed Somebody when Nobody did what Anybody could have.

- Anon

323. Be content with your lot; one cannot be first in everything.

- Aesop

324. There are wrinkles in time; folds that can be pushed to reveal what you may never have noticed but things that have always been there.

- Anon

325. I shall seize fate by the throat' it shall certainly never wholly overcome me.

- Ludwig von Beethoven

326. He who builds according to everyone else will have a crooked house.

- Anon

327. The antidote for fifty enemies is one friend.

- Aristotle

328. If you fail, fail again, fail better.

- Samuel Beckett

329. What ought a man to be? Well, my short answer is "himself."

- Henrik Ibsen

330. If something doesn't work, it is the solution to another problem.

- Robert Dilts

331. I take a simple view of life' keep your eye open and get on with it.

- Laurence Olivier

332. Make everything as simple as possible, but not simpler.

- Albert Einstein

333. See the things that you want as already yours. Think of them as yours, as belonging to you, as already in possession.

- Robert Collier

334. The world is a dangerous place to live; not because of the people who are evil, but because of the people who don't do anything about it.

- Albert Einstein

335. People give up with the first sign of failure not realizing that to fail means you have one less way to fail and you are one more step closer to a solution.

- Anon

336. To forget one's purpose is the commonest form of stupidity.

- Friedrich Nietzsche

337. To keep the body in good health is a duty or we shall not be able to keep our mind strong.

- Buddha

338. Fate is not written in huge brush strokes but in the tiniest detail, missing a train, getting up too late or too early, not going to that "insignificant" meeting. It can be anywhere, even in places we would never suspect.

- Anon

339. Give me a stock clerk a goal and I'll give you a man who will make history. Give me a man with no goals and I'll give you a stock clerk.

- J.C. Penne

340. Two people set off for the South Pole. One of them goes in the wrong direction but even though it takes him an extremely long time to get to his destination, he gets there before the other man. Why? Because the other man never left.

- Anon

341. Reading, after a certain age, diverts the mind too much from its creative pursuits. Any man who reads too much and uses his own brain too little falls into lazy habits of thinking.

- Albert Einstein

342. You can't fail every time.

- Anon

343. A man's reach should exceed his grasp or what is heaven for?
- Robert Browning

344. Sometimes, you just have to go with a fall in life. Allowing it to happen will hurt less.
- Anon

345. If your enemy is superior, evade him. If angry, irritate him. If equally matched, fight, and if not split and re-evaluate.
- Sun Tzu

346. At the end of the day, think about the events of the day. If anything didn't go the way you wanted, replay them in a way that thrills you. As you recreate these, you clean up the frequency from the day and you are emitting a new signal and frequency for tomorrow.
- Neville Goddard

347. She would rather light a candle than curse the darkness.
- Adlai Stevenson

348. It's not the mountain to climb that's hard but the pebble in your shoe.
- Muhammed Ali

349. There is a power in peace, a minority is only powerless if they conform to the majority.
- Anon

350. A teacher affects eternity, he can never tell where his influence stops.
- Henry Brooks Adams

351. We know more than we think we do.
- Benjamin Spock

352. The road up and road down are one and the same.
- Anon

353. The value of life lies not in the length of days but in the use you make of them.
- Montaigne

354.   Whereas then a rattle is a suitable occupation for infant children, education serves as a rattle for young person when older.

- Aristotle

355.   All experience is an arch to build upon.

- Henry Brooks Adams

356.   Good judgement comes from experience; bad judgement comes from poor or little experience.

- Anon

357.   The secret of happiness is to admire without desiring.

- F.H. Bradley

358.   The key to love is this; love someone too good for you and then make yourself better so that you deserve them.

- Zechariah Williams

359.   In a word, everything that we choose we choose for the sake of something else – except happiness which is an end.

- Aristotle

360.   Don't be like a Porsche car stuck in garage afraid that it will get scratched.

- Anon

361.   Sometimes a cause can be good even if the founder is corrupt.

- Anon

362.   It is the supreme art of the teacher to awaken joy in creative expression and knowledge.

- Albert Einstein

363.   The only place where success comes before work is the dictionary.

- Anon

364.   In skating over thin ice, our safety is in our speed

- Ralph Emerson

365.   One success can overshadow all failures.

- Anon

366.   Good habits formed at youth make all the difference.

- Aristotle

367.   Any man who can drive safely while kissing a pretty girl is simply not giving the kiss the attention it deserves.

- Albert Einstein

368.   Every child is an artist.

- Pablo Picasso

369.   The best way to destroy an enemy is to make him your friend.

- Tevur Proctor

370.   The best thing to do with your enemies is to bury your differences rather than each other.

- Anon

371.   Nothing is particularly hard if you break it into small jobs

- Henry Ford

372.   That which grows rapidly withers, that which grows slowly, endures.

- J.C. Holland

373.   I should always play fair when holding the winning cards.

- Oscar Wilde

374.   Mere cleverness is not wisdom.

- Euripides

375.   Invention is not limited to things we can hold in our hands. You can invent ideas.

- Anon

376.   Children are remarkable for their intelligence and ardor, for their curiosity, their intolerance of shams, the clarity and ruthlessness of their visions.

- Aldous Huxley

377.   How much could man have excelled had he chosen to rein in his cleverness rather than indulge it.

- Quintilian

378. Music is essentially useless, as life is' but both have an ideal extension which lends utility to its condition.

- George Santayana

379. After silence, that which comes nearest to expressing the inexpressible is music.

- Aldous Huxley

380. You are a human being, not a human doing.

- John Bradshaw

381. You can never cross the ocean until you have the courage to lose sight of the shore.

- Christopher Columbus

382. Every now and then, a man's mind is stretched by a new idea or sensation, and never shrinks back to its former dimensions.

- Oliver Wendell Holmes

383. There is no point in just borrowing ideas. We can't just be spouting old theories and borrowed themes.

- Anon

384. Logic will get you from A to B. Imagination will take you everywhere.

- Albert Einstein

385. Ideas can be impersonated, but only once can they be given freely.

- Anon

386. Make an idea only you can make.

- Anon

387. Any truth is better than indefinite doubt.

- Arthur Conan Doyle

388. From principles is derived probability, but truth or certainty is obtained only from facts.

- Tom Stoppard

389. He who cannot be a good follower cannot be a good leader.

- Aristotle

390.	Hope is definitely not the same thing as optimism. It is not the conviction that something will turn out well, but the certainty that something makes sense, regardless of how it turns out.

- Vaclav Havel

391.	All living things fear beating with clubs. All living things fear being put to death. Putting oneself in the place of the other, let no one kill nor cause another to kill.

- Dhammapada

392.	Education is what remains after one has forgotten what one has learned in school.

- Albert Einstein

393.	Above all, a query letter is a sales pitch and it is the single most important page an unpublished writer will ever write. It's the first impression and will either open the door or close it.

- Nicholas Sparks

394.	It is a capital mistake to theorize before one has data.

- Arthur Conan Doyle

395.	People of quality know everything without ever having been taught anything.

- Moliere

396.	You are a human being, not a human performance.

- John Bradshaw

397.	What lies beyond us and what lies before us are tiny matters when compared to what lies within us.

- Ralph Waldo Emerson

398.	Either you run the day or the day runs you.

- Jim Rohn

399.	The important thing is not to obtain facts as to discover ways of thinking about them.

- William Bragg

400.	No one can make you feel inferior without your consent.

- Eleanor Roosevelt

401. If there's no inner peace, people can't give it to you. The husband can't give it to you. Your children can't give it to you. You have to give it to you.

- Linda Evans

402. Let every nation know, whether it wishes us well or ill, that we shall pay any price, bear any burden, meet any hardship, support any friend, oppose any foe to assure the survival and the success of liberty.

- John F. Kennedy

403. All this will not be finished in the first 100 days. Nor will it be finished in the first 1,000 days, nor in the life of this Administration, nor even perhaps in the lifetime on this planet. But let us begin.

- John F. Kennedy

404. There is a statue inside every block of stone.

- George Orwell

405. Trust your instinct to the end, though you can render no reason.

- Ralph Waldo Emerson

406. An intellectual is someone whose mind watches itself.

- Albert Camus

407. We learn an art or craft by doing the things that we shall have to do when we have learnt it.

- Aristotle

408. All meanings depend on interpretation.

- George Eliot

409. There's a grain of sense in all absurdity and a grain of absurdity in all sense.

- Anon

410. All things are subject to interpretation; whichever interpretation prevails at a given time is a function of power and not truth.

- Friedrich Nietzsche

411. There is nothing more deceptive than an obvious fact.

- Arthur Conan Doyle

412. No more things should be presumed to exist than are absolutely necessary.

- William of Occam

413. Don't waste time on jealousy. Sometimes, you're ahead, sometimes you're behind.

- Mary Schmich

414. When a pair of magpies fly together,
They do not envy the pair of phoenixes.

- Lady Ho

415. Those who lack the courage will always find a philosophy to justify it.

- Albert Camus

416. Experience is not what happens to you; it's what you do with what happens to you.

- Aldous Huxley

417. Nature makes us human. Our actions decide whether we become monsters or maintain our claims to humanity.

- Anon

418. Goods have been classified under three heads, as a) external b) the soul c) of the body

- Aristotle

419. The superior man understands righteousness, the inferior man understands profit.

- Anon

420. Intellectual growth should commence at birth and cease only at death.

- Albert Einstein

421. The race is not to the swift or the battle to the strong nor does food come to the wise or wealth to the brilliant or favor to the learned but time and chance happen to us all.

- Anon

422. To do nothing is a decision.

- Anon

423. If you suffer a setback or disappointment, put your head down and plow ahead.

- Les Brown

424. The reading of good books is like a conversation with the best men of past centuries – in fact like a prepared conversation, in which they reveal only the best of their thoughts.

- Rene Descartes

425. If you don't want to work, you have to work up enough money until you don't have to work.

- Ogden Nash

426. The first problem for all of us, men and women is not to learn but to unlearn.

- Gloria Steinem

427. We are drowning in information but starved for knowledge.

- John Naisbitt

428. Most people aren't learning what they think they are learning. It's usually deeper.

- Ed Woodall

429. I don't think much of a man who is no wiser today than he was yesterday.

- Muhammad Ali

430. Most life experiences are not one-off lessons.

- Neville Carlyle Style

431. It is easier to live through someone else than to become complete yourself.

- Betty Friedan

432. Millions long for immortality who don't know what to do with themselves on a rainy Sunday afternoon.

- Susan Ertz

433. A person's life is his statement.

- Ezekiel

434. Most want to be remembered when they die. It's better to be remembered while you're alive.

- Anon

435. To be nameless in worthy deeds exceeds an infamous history.

- Sir Thomas Browne

436. Trying is more important than succeeding.

- Anon

437. If there's walls in your life stopping you, it is of no consequence. Walls can be knocked down.

- Anon

438. Never give up after a single attempt.

- Anon

439. Which is better: live long or live? Life is more than just avoiding death.

- Anon

440. A house unkempt is not as bad as a house unlived.

- Anon

441. Life is like swimming. You have to keep moving or you sink.

- Anon

442. Life is a play without a script, with us mprovising as best we can while being criticized by everybody.

- Anon

443. Any living thing that tries to stand still in the evolving flow of time becomes mechanical and thus comical in action.

- Henri Berguson

444. If life doesn't have that little bit of danger about it, you'd better create it. If life hands you that danger, accept it gratefully.

- Anthony Quayle

445. Trying to enjoy life too much speeds up ending it.

- Anon

446.   Limitations are primarily in the software, not the hardware.

- Dr. Wilson van Dusen

447.   Believing that the limits have already been set before we have a chance to get near them will ensure that we never perform to our full potential.

-   Anon

448.   All of the most successful people have sat on the cusp of failure at some point. They balance on the wall of limitations—one side holds success; the other holds failure. They play a dangerous game, but playing it is the way to win.

-   Anon

449.   To go too far is the same as not to go far enough.

- William Congreve

450.   A mind all logic is like a knife all blade. It makes the hand bleed that uses it.

-   Rabindranath Tagore

451.   Affection is responsible for nine-tenths of whatever solid and durable happiness there is in our lives.

-   C.S. Lewis

452.   You can't hold a man down without staying down with him.

- Booker T. Washington

453.   Immature love says I love you because I need you. Mature love says I need you because I love you.

-   Erich Froom

454.   Love only seems blind because the heart is infinitely capable of seeing things the eye cannot see.

-   Anon

455.   Without friends, no one would choose to live though he had all other goods.

-   Aristotle

456.   Even in a time of elephantine vanity and greed, one never has to look far to see the campfires of gentle people.

-   Garrison Keillor

457.   Life is made up of desires that seem big and vital one minute and little and absurd the next. I guess we get what's best for us in the end.

- Alice Caldwell Rice

458.   At the touch of love everyone becomes a poet.

- Plato

459.   I'm not going to change the way I look or the way I feel to conform to anything. I've always been a freak. So I've been a freak all my life and I have to live with that. I'm one of those people.

- John Lennon

460.   Every luxury must be paid for, and everything is a luxury, starting with being in this world.

- Cesare Pavese

461.   If we give power to negative things we could do it for positive thoughts as well.

- Lee Brower

462.   Expect everything and anything seems like nothing. Expect nothing and everything seems like everything.

- Samuel Hazo

463.   Age is a very high price to pay for maturity.

- Tom Stoppard

464.   Age' is the acceptance of a term of years. But maturity is the glory of years.

- Martha Graham

465.   Meditation is the soul's perspective glass.

- Owen Feltham

466.   Meditation is like a detox on your mind.

- Budai

467.   Meditation is the tongue of the soul and the language of our spirit.

- Jeremy Taylor

468. Yesterday is but today's memory, and tomorrow is today's dream.

- Khalil Gibran

469. The two most important days in your life are the day you are born and the day you find out why.

- Mark Twain

470. Your body hears everything your mind says.

- Naomi Judd

471. A healthy outside starts from the inside.

- Robert Urich

472. Life is all memory, except for the one present moment that goes by you so quickly you hardly catch it going.

- Tennessee Williams

473. There are three ways to learn from a mistake: hear of it, see it, do it.

- Anon

474. A blunder reveals an unsuspected world, and the individual is drawn into a relationship with forces that are not rightly understood. Mistakes are the result of the suppressed desires and conflicts. They are ripples on the surface of life, produced by unsuspected springs. The blunder may amount to the opening of a destiny.

- Joseph Campbell

475. Modesty is for the forgotten.

- Hector Berlioz

476. Never spend your money before you have earned it.

- Thomas Jefferson

477. A champion needs a motivation above and beyond winning.

- Pat Riley

478. Don't think. Thinking is the enemy of creativity. It's self-conscious, and anything self-conscious is lousy. You can't try to do things. You simply must do things.

- Ray Bradbury

479.   A lot of the fun lies in penetrating mystery.

- Anthony Hecht

480.   Refraining from pleasure cultivates temperance, and it is
through temperance that we can abstain from pleasure.

-   Aristotle

481.   I admire our ancestors, whoever they were. I think the first self-
conscious person must have shaken in his boots.
Because as he becomes self-conscious, he's no longer part of nature.
He sees himself against nature. He looks at the vastness of the
universe and it looks hostile.

- John Shelby Spong

482.   When you die, you can't take money with you. It's only
paper.

-   Anon

483.   No need being the richest man in a cemetery.

-   Anon

484.   It would not be too much to say that myth is the secret opening
through which the inexhaustible energies of the cosmos pour into
human cultural manifestation.

-   Joseph Campbell

485.   The mind loves the unknown. It loves images whose meaning is
unknown, since the meaning of the mind itself is unknown.

-   Rene Magritte

486.   People often say that motivation doesn't last. Well, neither does
bathing - that's why we recommend it daily.

- Zig Ziglar

487.   I know only that what is moral is what you feel good after and
what is immoral is what you feel bad after.

-   Ernest Hemingway

488.   Cowardice asks the question, "Is it safe?"
Expediency asks the question, "Is it politic?"
Vanity asks the question, "Is it popular?"
Conscience asks the question, "Is it right?"

- Martin Luther King

489. If you look at the world as it is, it will be what it is. If you look at what it could be, you will be motivated to change it.

- Anon

490. All the great legends are Templates for human behavior. I would define a myth as a story that has survived.

- John Boorman

491. The world is full of fools, and he who would see none should live alone and smash his mirror.

- Claude Le Petit

492. It is better to be high-spirited even though one makes more mistakes, than to be narrow-minded and all too prudent.

- Vincent Van Gogh

493. Some go through a forest without seeing firewood.

- Anon

494. The test of a first rate intelligence is the ability to hold two opposed ideas in the mind at the same time, and still retain the ability to function.

- F. Scott Fitzgerald

495. Just as treasures are uncovered from the earth, so virtue appears from good deeds, and wisdom appears from a pure and peaceful mind. To walk safely through the maze of human life, one needs the light of wisdom and the guidance of virtue.

- Buddha

496. Men take only their needs into consideration - never their abilities.

- Napoleon Bonaparte

497. A good decision is based on knowledge and not on numbers.

- Plato

498. You will never find the answer until you stop asking why you can't do something and start figuring out how you will.

- Mark Hooper

499. If you are going through hell, keep going.

- Winston Churchill.

500.   From the astrologer came the astronomer, from the alchemist the chemist, from the mesmerist the experimental psychologist. The quack of yesterday is the professor of tomorrow.

- Arthur Conan Doyle

501.   Rooms don't change, ornaments stand where you place them, only the heart decays.

- Graham Greene

502.   People go on about "back in my day," but our days are today, and that's what's going to make a difference, more than anything in the past.

-   Anon

503.   If you go for an audition, there will be hundreds of people who have more experience, who are better looking, more well connected, more suited to the part and more talented. So you're probably not going to get it. But you are definitely not going to get it if you don't go.

- Robert De Niro

504.   Whatever you can do, or dream you can, begin it. Boldness has genius, power and magic in it.

-   Johann Wolfgang von Goethe

505.   That men do not learn very much from the lessons of history is the most important of all the lessons of history.

-   Aldous Huxley

506.   There was a reviewer a while back who wrote that my pictures didn't have any beginning or any end. He didn't mean it as a compliment, but it was.

-   Jackson Pollack

507.   We need to give each other the space to grow, to be ourselves, to exercise our diversity.

-   Max de Pree

508.   The brain's calculations do not require our conscious effort, only our attention and our openness to let the information through.

-   Marilyn Ferguson

509. When two opposite points of view are expressed with equal force the truth does not necessarily lie midway between them. It is possible for one side to be simply wrong. And that justifies passion on the other side.

- Anon

510. There are no absolute truths. All claims are relative, even this one.

- Anon

511. Opinion is ambiguity. It's not how things are. It's how we feel things are.

- Anon

512. Opinions can be more powerful than facts.

- Anon

513. Tomorrow's good old days are happening now.

- Anon

514. Most of what matters in your life take place in your absence.
- Salman Rushdie

515. Opportunities multiply as they are seized.

- Anon

516. Difficulties mastered are opportunities won.
- Winston Churchill

517. Punishment may make us obey the orders we are given, but at best it will only teach an obedience to authority, not a self-control which enhances our self-respect.
- Bruno Bettelheim

518. God gives every bird a worm, but he doesn't throw it into the nest.

- Anon

519. No one thing is the root to anything.
- Richard Dawkins

520. The best revenge is massive success.
- Frank Sinatra

521. The thing you fear most has no power. Your fear of it is what has the power.

- Oprah Winfrey

522. All difficult things have their origin in that which is easy, and great things in that which is small.

- Lao Tzu

523. How true Daddy's words were when he said: children must look after their own upbringing. Parents can only give good advice or put them on the right paths, but the final forming of a person's character lies in their own hands.

- Anne Frank

524. It's not childish to devote oneself to a craft rather than a career, to an idea rather than an institution.

- David Mamet

525. The past is what provides us with the building blocks. Our job today is to create new buildings out of them.

- Theodore Zeldin

526. Life shrinks or expands in proportion to one's courage.

- Anais Nin

527. If a man hasn't discovered something he will die for, he isn't fit to live.

- Martin Luther King

528. To have a new vision of the future, it has always first been necessary to have a new vision of the past.

- Theodore Zeldin

529. If you can't change the past, take responsibility for it.

- Anon

530. Who looks outside, dreams;
Who looks inside, awakens.

- Carl Jung

531. We need the courage to be imperfect.

- Sofie Lazarsfeld

532.   Chess helps you develop patience and discipline in choosing between alternatives when an impulsive decision seems attractive.
- Stanley Kubrick

533.   Give me 6 hours to chop down a tree and I will spend the first 4 hours sharpening the axe.
- Abraham Lincoln

534.   I've learned you can make a mistake and the whole world doesn't end.
- Lisa Kudrow

535.   Some think people are great persuaders because they are born that way. None of us are born talking. Great persuaders are great listeners.
- Anon

536.   Persuasion is better than force.
- Mahatma Gandhi

537.   Fear is not a lasting teacher of duty.
- Marcus Tullius Cicero

538.   As soon as the fear approaches near, attack and destroy it.
- Chanakya

539.   You shall know the truth and the truth shall make you mad.
- Aldous Huxley

540.   Forget your personal tragedy. We are all bitched from the start and you especially have to be hurt like hell. But when you get the damned hurt, use it-don't cheat with it.
- Ernest Hemingway

541.   The food you eat can be either the safest and most powerful form of medicine or the slowest form of poison.
- Ann Wigmore

542.   Happiness is the setting of the soul into its most appropriate spot.
- Aristotle

543.   In making a speech one must study three points: first, the means of producing persuasion; second, the language; third the proper arrangement of the various parts of the speech.

- Aristotle

544.   A good plan violently executed now is better than a perfect plan executed next week.

- George S. Patton

545.   The more you plan, the more you can adapt to setbacks.

-   Anon

546.   Constructive criticism is better than praise.

-   Anon

547.   If you fail to plan, you plan to fail.

-   George S. Patton

548.   The dream begins with a teacher who believes in you, who pushes and leads you to the next plateau, sometimes poking you with a sharp stick called "truth".

-   Dan Rather

549.   With Positive Mental Attitude, failure is a learning experience, a rung on the ladder, a plateau at which to get your thoughts in order and prepare to try again.

-   W. Clement Stone

550.   Don't just plan for success. Plan for failure.

-   Anon

551.   There can be a vast gap between what we cannot do, what others believe we cannot do and what others convince us we cannot do. And often there is.

-   Anon

552.   Each player must accept the cards life deals him or her: but once they are in hand, he or she alone must decide how to play the cards in order to win the game.

-   Voltaire

553.   A manager has his cards dealt to him and he must play them.
- Miller Huggins

554. Everyone has inside of him a piece of good news.

- Anne Frank

555. The most valuable of all education is the ability to make yourself do the thing you have to do, when it has to be done, whether you like it or not.

- Aldous Huxley

556. The world is ALWAYS getting better but we always think it's getting worse.

- Penn Jilette

557. Continuous effort, not intelligence is the key to unlocking our potential.

- Winston Churchill

558. Power doesn't corrupt; the fear of a loss of power does.

- John Steinbeck

559. Everything we hear is an opinion, not a fact. Everything we see is a perspective, not the truth.

- Marcus Aurelius

560. Meditation is the soul's perspective glass.

- Owen Feltham

561. Fame is a vapor, popularity an accident, and riches take wings. Only one thing endures and that is character.

- Horace Greeley

562. Great things are not accomplished by those who yield to trends, fads and popular opinion.

- Jack Kerouac

563. If all of us acted in unison as I act individually there would be no wars and no poverty. I have made myself personally responsible for the fate of every human being who has come my way.

- Anais Nin

564. Beauty is worse than wine, it intoxicates both the holder and the beholder.

- Aldous Huxley

565.   I hope our wisdom will grow with our power, and teach us, that the less we use our power the greater it will be.

- Thomas Jefferson

566.   The study and knowledge of the universe would somehow be lame and defective were no practical results to follow.

- Marcus Tullius Cicero

567.   Your smile will give you a positive countenance that will make people feel comfortable around you.

- Les Brown

568.   Life is too short to stuff a mushroom.

- Shirley Conran

569.   There are things known and there are things unknown, and in between are the doors of perception.

- Aldous Huxley

570.   Make yourself useful to something and to someone.

- Ralph Emerson

571.   Prayer indeed is good, but while calling on the gods a man should himself lend a hand.

- Hippocrates

572.   Prayer should not be a substitute for action.

- Anon

573.   An ounce of practice is worth more than tons of preaching.

- Mahatma Gandhi

574.   I feel that luck is preparation meeting opportunity.

- Oprah Winfrey

575.   The best preparation for good work tomorrow is to do good work today.

- Elbert Hubbard

576.   You can't run with the hare and hunt with the hounds.

- Anon

577. The only thing worse than being out while opportunity comes to your door is to be in and not bother to answer.

- Anon

578. Courage is grace under pressure.

- Ernest Hemingway

579. The Good of man is the active exercise of his soul's faculties in conformity with excellence or virtue.

- Aristotle

580. The wish for healing has always been half of the battle.

- Lucius Annaeus Seneca

581. Never argue with an idiot. They will drag you down to their level and beat you with experience.

- Anon

582. The very best thing for a person is health
Second good looks and third honest wealth,
The fourth to be in the prime of your life
With people around you who cause no strife.

- Plato Gorgias

583. Any reaction is better than none.

- Gavin Rossdale

584. Nobody can hurt me without my permission.

- Mahatma Gandhi

585. Stone walls don't make a prison nor iron bars a cage.

- Anon

586. The meeting of two personalities is like the contact of two chemical substances; if there is any reaction, both are transformed.

- Carl Jung

587. To travel is to discover that everyone is wrong about other countries.

- Aldous Huxley

588. The tragedy of racism is we are all human.

- Anon

589. Rationality is ineffective against the irrational. The only thing that works is fear.

- Alec Baldwin

590. It doesn't matter if a cat is black or white, as long as it catches mice.

– Deng Xiaoping

591. When I am getting ready to reason with a man, I spend one-third of my time thinking about myself and what I am going to say and two-thirds about him and what he is going to say.

- Abraham Lincoln

592. Our intention creates our reality.

- Wayne Dyer

593. I'm always ready to learn, although I do not always like being taught.

- Winston Churchill

594. We can't solve problems by using the same kind of thinking we used when we created them.

- Albert Einstein

595. Betrayal is the only truth that sticks.

- Arthur Miller

596. To raise new questions, new possibilities, to regard old problems from a new angle, requires imagination and marks real advance in science.

- Albert Einstein

597. You can design and create, and build the most wonderful place in the world. But it takes people to make the dream a reality.

- Walt Disney

598. Age wrinkles the body.
Quitting wrinkles the soul.

- Douglas MacArthur

599. You miss 100% of the chances not taken.

- Wayne Gretzky

600. Many of life's failures are people who did not realize how close they were to success when they gave up.

- Thomas Edison

601. Winners never quit; quitters never win.

- Anon

602. Truth is everybody is going to hurt you, you've just gotta find the ones worth suffering for.

- Bob Marley

603. One should always have one's boots on, and be ready to leave.

- Montaigne

604. Simplicity is prerequisite for reliability.

- Edsger Dijkstra

605. Divide each and every difficulty into as many parts as is feasible and necessary to resolve it.

- Rene Descartes

606. A reputation for a thousand years may depend upon the conduct of a single moment.

- Ernest Bramah

607. If I can see an ending, I can work backward.

- Arthur Miller

608. I have never accepted what many people have kindly said – namely, that I inspired the nation... It was the nation and the race dwelling all round the globe that had the lion's heart. I had the luck to be called upon to give the roar. I also hope that I sometimes suggested to the lion the right place to use his claws.

- Winston Churchill

609. Never doubt that a small group of committed people can change the world, indeed it's the only thing that ever has.

- Margaret Mead

610. Responsibility will not fit in our hands. It must be shouldered.

- Anon

611. We can't be expected to do every job. But we expect every job to be done.

- Anon

612. The right time is any time that one is still so lucky as to have.

- Henry James

613. Life is about timing.

- Carl Lewis

614. If you are going to be a sheep, make sure you know who your shepherd is.

- Anon

615. A hero is an ordinary individual who finds the strength to persevere and endure in spite of overwhelming obstacles.

- Christopher Reeve

616. I am a part of all that I have met.

- F. Scott Fitzgerald

617. Determination gives you the resolve to keep going in spite of the roadblocks that lay before you.

- Denis Waitley

618. Do not underestimate the determination of a quiet man.

- Iain Duncan Smith

619. Better to wear out than to rust out.

- Richard Cumberland

620. The afternoon of human life must also have a significance of its own and cannot be merely a pitiful appendage to life's morning.

- Carl Jung

621. People mistake limitation for high standards.

- Jean Toomer

622. Keep up the old standards, and day by day raise them higher.

- John Wanamaker

623. It's not stress that kills, it is our reaction to it.

- Hans Selye

624. Many are stubborn in pursuit of the path they have chosen, few in pursuit of the goal.

- Friedrich Nietzsche

625. The greatest virtues are those which are most useful to other people.

- Aristotle

626. If you fail to plant desires in your subconscious mind, it will feed upon the thoughts which reach it as the result of your neglect.

- Napoleon Hill

627. Within psychology and neuroscience, some new and rigorous experimental paradigms for studying consciousness have helped it begin to overcome the stigma that has been attached to the topic for most of this century.

- David Chalmers

628. The victory is in preparation.

- Winston Churchill

629. What is our aim?.... Victory, victory at all costs, victory in spite of all terror, victory, however long and hard the road may be; for without victory, there can be no survival.

- Winston Churchill

630. Today, certain people file for bankruptcy, and it no longer has the stigma it once had. Now it's almost considered wise, a way to regroup and come back again.

- David Dinkins

631. We should behave to our friends as we would them to behave to us.

- Aristotle

632. Never do to others what you wouldn't want them to do to you.

- Jesus Christ

633. Never impose on others what you would not choose for yourself.

- Confucius

634. Hurt no one so that no one may hurt you.

- Muhammad

635. Do as you would be done by.

- Anon

636. Put others first.

- Confucius

637. 'Tis not enough to help the feeble up, but to support them after.
- William Shakespeare

638. Truth stands, even if there be no public support. It is self-sustained.

- Mahatma Gandhi

639. A constant struggle, a ceaseless battle to bring success from inhospitable surroundings, is the price of all great achievements.
- Orison Swett Marden

640. All we are is a lot of talking nitrogen.

- Arthur Miller

641. It was only from an inner calm that man was able to discover and shape calm surroundings.

- Stephen Gardiner

642. People need dramatic examples to shake them out of apathy and I can't do that as a man, I can be destroyed but as a symbol I can be incorruptible, I can be everlasting.

- Bruce Wayne
(Batman Begins)

643. Symbols are not manufactured; they cannot be ordered, invented or permanently suppressed. They are spontaneous productions of the psyche, and each bears within it, undamaged, the germ power of its source.

- Joseph Campbell

644. You can be better than your technique.

- Dave Brubeck

645. The government is not an evil force. It's like any mass assemblage—a group of the willing, chosen from the fit, to do the necessary.

- Anon

646. Those who expect to reap the blessings of freedom must undergo the fatigue of supporting it.

- Anon

647. Talent wins games, teamwork wins championships.

- Michael Jordan

648. Laughter can help relieve tension in even the heaviest of matters.

- Allen Klein

649. Always trust your team mates. No matter what. Or you have nothing.

- Eric Cantona

650. By concentrating on precision, one arrives at technique, but by concentrating on technique one does not arrive at precision.

- Bruno Walter

651. A person is not a vase to be filled, but a fire to be lit.

- Anon

652. I think everyone should sit down and write a book. It's a lot like therapy but a lot less expensive.

- Norma McCorvey

653. Happiness can exist only in acceptance.

- George Orwell

654. Wit is the salt of conversation, not the food.

- Anon

655. Acceptance of what has happened is the first step to overcoming the consequences of any misfortune.

- William James

656. Give us the tools and we will get the job done.

- Winston Churchill

657. Heaven knows we need never be ashamed of our tears for they are pain upon the blinding dust of Earth overlaying our hard hearts.
- Charles Dickens

658. A man travels the world in search of what he needs and returns home to find it.
- George Moore

659. What an odd thing tourism is. You fly off to a strange land, eagerly abandoning all the comforts of home, and then expend vast quantities of time and money in a largely futile attempt to recapture the comforts that you wouldn't have lost if you hadn't left home in the first place.
- Bill Bryson

660. A life lived of choice is a life of conscious action. A life lived of chance is a life of unconscious creation.
- Neale Donald Walsch

661. Forget mind over matter. A better phrase is mind and matter in unity.
- Tom Ryan

662. Everybody likes a kidder, but nobody lends him money.
- Arthur Miller

663. All forms of self-defeating behavior are unseen and unconscious, which is why their existence is denied.
- Vernon Howard

664. The crown of life is neither happiness nor annihilation, it is understanding.
- Winifred Holtby

665. The dust of exploded beliefs may make a fine sunset.
- Geoffrey Madan

666. We need to live in a world with nothing else to conquer.
- Anon

667. Violence is a language you force others to learn because you don't know how to communicate any other way.
- Anon

668. Some people claim to fight so we don't have to fight. Fighting for peace or respect or honor puts us at the opposing side of our intentions.

- Anon

669. Only the weak succumb to brutality. Fights start over ideas, then morals, then people, then ownership, and then countries, but we are always fighting over the same thing—nothing.

- Anon

670. Meet with open arms, not thrashing fists.

- Anon

671. The supreme act of war is to subdue the enemy without fighting.

- Sun Tzu

672. Force is never a remedy.

- Anon

673. Be silent unless your speech is better than silence.

- Salvator Rosa

674. In the end, it all comes to choices to turn stumbling blocks into stepping stones.

- Amber Frey

675. Victorious warriors win first and then go to war. Defeated warriors go to war first and then seek to win.

- Sun Tzu

676. When weak, pretend to be strong.
When strong, pretend to be weak.

- Sun Tzu

677. Although men are accused of not knowing their own weakness, yet perhaps few know their own strength.

- Jonathan Swift

678. The first wealth is health.

- Ralph Waldo Emerson

679. The greatest revolution of our generation is the discovery that human beings, by changing the inner attitudes of their minds, can change the outer aspects of their lives.

- William James

680. Your mind is not in your way.

- Cus D'Amato

681. The whole is more than the sum of the parts.

- Aristotle

682. The price of wisdom is beyond rubies.

- Anon

683. Where there is no perception, appellation, conception, or conventional expression; there one speaks of "perfect wisdom."

- Mahayana Buddhist texts

684. Live in contact with dreams and you will get something of their charm. Live in contact with facts and you will get something of their brutality. I wish I could find a country to live where the facts were not so brutal and the dreams not unreal.

- George Bernard Shaw
(John Bulls Other Island)

685. Do more of what you love and less of everything else.

- Cameron Johnson

686. You see things and say why but I dream of things that never were and say why not?

- George Bernard Shaw

687. All men by nature desire knowledge.

- Aristotle

688. Who's more foolish—the dreamer who dreams his life away, or the one so afraid to dream that he never even tries?

- Anon

689. Better than a thousand hollow words, is one word that brings peace.

- Buddha

690. If a man will begin with certainties, he shall end in doubts; but if he will be content to begin with doubts, he shall end in certainties.
- Francis Bacon

691. One man that has a mind and knows it can always beat ten men who haven't and don't.
- George Bernard Shaw

692. If you hear a voice within you say "you cannot paint" then by all means paint and that voice will be silenced.
- Vincent Van Gogh

693. Whatever words we utter should be chosen with care for people will hear them and be influenced by them for good or ill.
- Buddha

694. Neither a lofty degree of intelligence nor imagination nor both together go to the making of genius. Love, love, love that is the soul of genius.
- Nikolaus von Jacquin

695. Some books are to be tasted, others to be swallowed, and some few to be chewed and digested.
- Francis Sr.

696. An investment in knowledge pays the best interest.
- Benjamin Franklin

697. The quality of a person's life is in direct proportion to their commitment to excellence, regardless of their chosen field of endeavor.
- Vincent Lombardi

698. If you're trying to achieve, there will be roadblocks. I've had them; everybody has had them. But obstacles don't have to stop you. If you run into a wall, don't turn around and give up. Figure out how to climb it, go through it, or work around it.
- Michael Jordan

699. Ask and it will be given to you; search, and you will find, knock and the door will be opened for you.
- Jesus Christ

700. The only person you are destined to become is the person you decide to be.

- Ralph Waldo Emerson

701. When I was 5 years old, my mother always told me that happiness was the key to life. When I went to school, they asked me what I wanted to be when I grew up. I wrote down "happy." They told me I didn't understand the assignment, and I told them they didn't understand life.

- Anon

702. When I stand before God at the end of my life, I would hope that I would not have a single bit of talent left and could say, I used everything you gave me.

- Erma Bombeck

703. Certain things catch your eye, but pursue only those that capture the heart.

- Indian Proverb

704. Teach thy tongue to say, "I do not know" and thou shalt progress.

- Maimonides

705. Everything you've ever wanted is on the other side of fear.

- George Addair

706. Fall seven times and stand up eight.

- Japanese Proverb

707. Start where you are. Use what you have. Do what you can.
- Arthur Ashe

708. When one door of happiness closes, another opens, but often we look so long at the closed door that we do not see the one that has been opened for us.

- Helen Keller

709. Everything has beauty, but not everyone can see.

- Confucius

710.   How wonderful it is that nobody need wait a single moment
before starting to improve the world.

- Anne Frank

711.   When I let go of what I am, I become what I might be.

- Lao Tzu

712.   Happiness is not something readymade. It comes from your
own actions.

- Dalai Lama

713.   If you're offered a seat on a rocket ship, don't ask what seat!
Just get on.

- Sheryl Sandberg

714.   If the wind will not serve, take to the oars.

- Latin Proverb

715.   You can't fall if you don't climb. But there's no joy in living
your whole life on the ground.

- Anon

716.   We must believe that we are gifted for something, and that this
thing, at whatever cost, must be attained.

- Marie Curie

717.   Too many of us are not living our dreams because we are
living our fears.

- Les Brown

718.   Challenges are what make life interesting and overcoming
them is what makes life meaningful.

- Joshua J. Marine

719.   If you want to lift yourself up, lift up someone else.
- Booker T. Washington

720.   The game of basketball has been everything to me. My place
of refuge, place I've always gone where I needed comfort and
peace. It's been the site of intense pain and the most intense feeling
of joy and satisfaction. It's a relationship that has evolved over time.
- Michael Jordan

721.   Limitations live in our minds. If we use imagination, our possibilities become limitless.

-    Jamie Paolinetti

722.   I have been impressed with the urgency of doing. Knowing is not enough; we must apply. Being willing is not enough; we must do.

-    Leonardo da Vinci

723.   You take your life in your own hands, and what happens? A terrible thing, no one to blame.

-    Erica Jong

724.   What's money? A man is a success if he gets up in the morning and goes to bed at night and in between does what he wants to do.

-    Bob Dylan

725.   In order to succeed, your desire for success should be greater than your fear of failure.

- Anon

726.   A person who never made a mistake never tried anything new.

– Albert Einstein

727.   The person who says it cannot be done should not interrupt the person who is doing it.

– Chinese Proverb

728.   There are no traffic jams along the extra mile.

– Roger Staubach

729.   I would rather die of passion than of boredom.

-    Vincent van Gogh

730.   If you want your children to turn out well, spend twice as much time with them, and half as much money.

-    Abigail Van Buren

731.   Setting goals is the first step in turning the invisible into the visible.

-    Tony Robbins

732. It is not what you do for your children, but what you have taught them to do for themselves, that will make them successful human beings.

- Ann Landers

733. Build your own dreams, or someone else will hire you to build theirs.

- Farrah Gray

734. I can accept failure. I can't accept not trying.

- Michael Jordan

735. Stay committed to your decisions, but stay flexible in your approach.

- Tony Robbins

736. To effectively communicate, we must realize that we are all different in the way we perceive the world and use this understanding as a guide to our communication with others.

- Tony Robbins

737. There is no such thing as a perfect player, and I don't believe there is only one greatest player of anything either.

- Michael Jordan

738. Some people want it to happen, some wish it would happen, others make it happen.

- Michael Jordan

739. The battles that count aren't the ones for gold medals. The struggles within yourself – the invisible battles inside all of us – that's where it's at.

- Jesse Owens

740. I have learned over the years that when one's mind is made up, this diminishes fear.

- Rosa Parks

741. If you look at what you have in life, you'll always have more. If you look at what you don't have in life, you'll never have enough.

- Oprah Winfrey

742.   Education costs money. But then so does ignorance.

- Sir Claus Moser

743.   Remember that not getting what you want is sometimes a wonderful stroke of luck.

- Dalai Lama

744.   It's your place in the world; it's your life. Go on and do all you can with it, and make it the life you want to live.

- Mae Jemison

745.   You can't use up creativity. The more you use, the more you have.

- Maya Angelou

746.   A real decision is measured by the fact that you've taken a new action. If there's no action, you haven't truly decided.

- Tony Robbins

747.   What you do not bring forth will destroy you.

- Jesus Christ

748.   Our lives begin to end the day we become silent about things that matter.

- Martin Luther King

749.   Do what you can, where you are, with what you have.

- Teddy Roosevelt

750.   Dreaming, after all, is a form of planning.

- Gloria Steinem

751.   The secret of success is learning how to use pain and pleasure instead of having pain and pleasure use you. If you do that, you're in control of your life. If you don't, life controls you.

- Tony Robbins

752.   Dream big and dare to fail.

- Norman Vaughan

753.   You may be disappointed if you fail, but you are doomed if you don't try.

- Beverly Sills

754. The only limit to your impact is your imagination and commitment.

- Tony Robbins

755. Only those who have learned the power of sincere and selfless contribution experience life's deepest joy: true fulfillment.

- Tony Robbins

756. Life is what we make it, always has been, always will be.

- Grandma Moses

757. It's not the events of our lives that shapes us, but our beliefs as to what those events mean.

- Tony Robbins

758. The question isn't who is going to let me; it's who is going to stop me.

- Ayn Rand

759. When everything seems to be going against you, remember that the airplane takes off against the wind, not with it.

- Henry Ford

760. It's not the years in your life that count. It's the life in your years.

- Abraham Lincoln

761. Change your thoughts and you change your world.

- Norman Vincent Peale

762. The only way to do great work is to love what you do.

- Steve Jobs

763. If you can dream it, you can achieve it.

- Zig Ziglar

764. It is never too late to be what you might have been.

- George Eliot

765. If you do what you've always done, you'll get what you've always gotten.

- Tony Robbins

766. What we can or cannot do, what we consider possible or impossible, is rarely a function of our true capability. It is more likely a function of our beliefs about who we are.

- Tony Robbins

767. I think it's my adventure, and I guess my attitude is, let the chips fall where they may.

- Leonard Nimoy

768. The third-rate mind is only happy when it is thinking with the majority. The second-rate mind is only happy when it is thinking with the minority. The first-rate mind is only happy when it is thinking.

- A.A. Milne

769. Anytime I feel lost, I pull out a map and stare. I stare until I have reminded myself that life is a giant adventure, so much to do, to see.

- Angelina Jolie

770. When words become unclear, I shall focus with photographs. When images become inadequate, I shall be content with silence.

- Ansel Adams

771. You will never win if you never begin.

- Helen Rowland

772. I think, therefore I am.

- Rene Descartes

773. Sweat saves blood.

- Ervin Rommel

774. What's done is done.

- William Shakespeare

775. Poverty wants few things, avarice, everything.

- Bartholomew of San Concordio

776. Even a broken clock is right twice a day.

- Jim Butcher

777. To the uneducated, an A is just three sticks.

- A.A. Milne

778. Do things that have never been done.

- Russell A. Kirsch

779. A person who makes few mistakes makes little progress.

- Bryant McGill

780. An empty man is full of himself.

- Edward Abbey

781. An alert and learned man will take advice from any event.

- Ali bin Abu-Talib

782. Life seems but a quick succession of busy nothings.

- Jane Austen

783. Leave the world a little better than you found it.

- Robert Stephenson Smyth Baden-Powell

784. The best way to pay for a lovely moment is to enjoy it.

- Richard Bach

785. The more a man judges, the less he loves.

- Honor de Balzac

786. Whoever wants to reach a distant goal must take small steps.

- Saul Bellow

787. The mind is the reality. You are what you think.

- Alfred Bester

788. A goal is a dream with a deadline.

- Napoleon Hill

789. Trust opens up new and unimagined possibilities.

- Robert C. Solomon

790. To travel is to discover that everyone is wrong about other countries.

- Aldous Huxley

791. The secret of your future is hidden in your daily routine.
- Mike Murdock

792. Any place is a palace if your heart decides so.
- Tamil Proverb

793. The money from selling a dog doesn't show love.
- Tamil Proverb

794. Hope of ill gain is the beginning of loss.
- Democritus

795. Heroism is endurance for one moment more.
- George F. Kennan

796. Courage is being scared to death, but saddling up anyway.
- John Wayne

797. Failure defeats losers and inspires winners.
- Robert T. Kiyosaki

798. Poor people have a big T.V. Rich people have a big library.
- Jim Rohn

799. A lie has speed but truth has endurance.
- Edgar J. Mohn

800. It is not the mountain we conquer, but ourselves.
- Edmund Hillary
(First man to climb Mt. Everest)

801. Desire, like the atom, is explosive with creative force.
- Paul Vernon Buser

802. We make our own fortunes and we call them fate.
- Benjamin Disraeli

803. Be social to all, sociable to many, familiar to few.
- Benjamin Franklin

804. Every single success story begin with a dream.
- Anon

805. All things are difficult before they are easy.

                                       - Thomas Fuller

806. Difficulty is the excuse history never accepts.

                             - Edward R. Murrow

807. The aims of life are the best defense against death.

                                   - Primo Levi

808. We never know the worth of water till the well is dry.

                                       - Thomas Fuller

809. There are no passengers on spaceship earth. We are all crew.

                             - Marshall McLuhan

810. Difficulties are things that show a person what they are.

                                   - Epictetus

811. No one has ever learned fully to know themselves.

                             - Johann von Goethe

812. No great discovery was ever made without a bold guess.

                                 - Isaac Newton

813. When the stomach is full, it is easy to talk of fasting.

                                   - St. Jerome

814. Better a witty fool than foolish wit.

                           - William Shakespeare

815. If you can't do what you want, do what you can.

                             - Lois McMaster Bujold

816. Proverbs are always platitude until you have personally
experienced the truth of them.

                                 - Aldous Huxley

817. Men may move mountains, but ideas move men.

                             - Lois McMaster Bujold

818. Any plan is bad which is not susceptible of change.

                         - Bartholomew of San Concordio

819. Kill your doubt with confidence.

          - Brandon Boyd

820. Genius does what it must. Talent does what it can.

          - Robert Bulwer Lytton

821. A good heart is better than all the heads in the world.

          - Edward George Earl Bulwer Lytton

822. Width of life is greater than length of life.

          - Avicenna

823. A wise man will make more opportunities, than he finds.

          - Francis Bacon

824. Think like a man of action, act like a man of thought.

          - Henry-Louis Bergson

825. There's nothing impossible to him who tries.

          - Alexander III

826. Those who see the invisible can do the impossible.

          - Pandurang Shastri Vaijnath Athavale

827. Awareness without action is worthless.

          - Phil McGraw

828. Wisdom is the anticipation of consequences.

          - Norman Cousins

829. Life is pain and the enjoyment of love is an anesthetic.

          - Cesare Pavese

830. Man is free at the moment he wishes to be.

          - Voltaire

831. Never confuse trust with familiarity.

          - Robert C. Solomon

832. Many argue, not many converse.

          - Louisa May Alcott

833. My best friend is the man who in wishing me well wishes it for my sake.

- Aristotle

834. The less routine, the more life.

- Amon Bronson Alcott

835. Victory is sweetest when you've known defeat.

- Malcolm S. Forbes

836. The love we give away is the only love we keep.

- Elbert Hubbard

837. Nothing is so difficult as not deceiving oneself.

- Ludwig Wittgenstein

838. A well-aimed spear is worth three.

- Tamil Proverb

839. Tough times never last, but tough people do.

- Robert H. Schuller

840. Grace is to the body; what good manners are to the mind.

- Francois de la Rochefoucauld

841. Be content to act and leave the talking to others.

- Balthasa

842. To the artist, there is never anything ugly in nature.

- Auguste Rodin

843. In the middle of difficulty lies opportunity.

- Anon

844. Fatigue is the physical confirmation of superior effort.

- Wes Fessler

845. The eyes sees only what the mind is prepared to comprehend.

- Henry Bergson

846. Fortune is the rod of the weak, and the staff of the brave.

- James Russell Lowell

847. Wisdom becomes nonsense in the mouth of a fanatic.
- Otto Schudrmer

848. The greatest inspiration is often born of desperation.
- Comer Cotrell

849. The truth needs so little rehearsal.
- Barbara Kingsolver

850. It is the mark of an educated mind to be able to entertain a thought without accepting it.
- Aristotle

851. The best way to escape from a problem is to solve it.
- Alan Saporta

852. A little flattery will support a man through great fatigue.
- James Munroe

853. The lowest ebb is the turn of the tide.
- Henry Wadsworth Longfellow

854. No day but today.
- Jonathan Larson

855. Love conquers all.
- Virgil

856. Hope springs eternal.
- Alexander Pope

857. Seize the day.
- Horace

858. Without self-discipline, there is no success.
- Anon

859. Attitude is everything.
- Charles Swindoll

860. The first step to getting the things you want out of life is this: Decide what you want.
- Ben Stein

861.   Life is far too important a thing ever to talk seriously about.
                                              -   Oscar Wilde

862.   Life is a long lesson in humility.
                                              -   James M Barrie

863.   The secret of a good life is to have the right loyalties and hold
        them in the right scale of values.
                                              -   Norman Thomas

864.   The purpose of life is to fight maturity.
                                              -   Dick Werthimer

865.   Not a shred of evidence exists in favor of the idea that life is
        serious.
                                              -   Brendan Gill

866.   We make a living by what we get, we make a life by what we
        give.
                                              -   Sir Winston Churchill

867.   Life is an unbroken succession of false situations.
                                              -   Thornton Wilder

868.   Life is something that everyone should try at least once.
                                              -   Henry J. Tillman

869.   Enjoy your life without comparing it to others.
                                              -   Condobcet

870.   The truth is more important than the facts.
                                              -   Frank Lloyd Wright

871.   Never stop questioning.
                                              -   Albert Einstein

872.   Only those who dare to fail greatly can ever achieve greatly.
                                              -   Robert F. Kennedy

873.   Thinking will not overcome fear but action will.
                                              -   W. Clement Stone

874. The most wasted of all days is one without laughter.
- E.E. Cummings

875. Facts do not cease to exist because they are ignored.
- Aldous Huxley

876. A creative man is motivated by the desire to achieve, not by the desire to beat others.
- Ayn Rand

877. If you aren't fired with enthusiasm, you will be fired with enthusiasm.
- Vince Lombardi

878. Fantastic things happen—to the way we feel, to the way we make other people feel. All this simply by using positive words.
- Professor Leo F Buscaglia

879. As one person, I cannot change the world, but I can change the world of one person.
- Paul Shane Spear

880. If you don't know where you are going you will probably end up somewhere else.
- Laurence Peter

881. The greatest revenge is to accomplish what others say you cannot do.
- Anon

882. All glory comes from daring to begin.
- Eugene F. Ware

883. I'd rather be optimistic and a fool, than pessimistic and right.
- Anon

884. Once you have a clear picture of your priorities—that, is values, goals, and high leverage activities - organize around them.
- Stephen Covey

885. No one is useless in this world who lightens the burdens of another.
- Charles Dickens

886.   The reason many people don't see things in the right
perspective is that they are always looking for an angle.

- Anon

887.   Kind words echoes are truly endless.

- Mother Teresa

888.   Our aspirations are our responsibilities.

- Robert Browning

889.   Confidence comes not from always being right, but from not
feeling being wrong.

- Peter McIntyre

890.   Leave the past, engage the present, create the future.

- Julio Melara

891.   At his best, man is the noblest of all animals; separated from
law and justice he is the worse.

- Aristotle

892.   My mind rebels at stagnation. Give me problems, give me
work, give me the most abstruse cryptogram, or the most intricate
analysis, and I am in my own proper atmosphere. But I abhor the
dull routine of existence. I crave for mental exaltation.

- Arthur Conan Doyle

893.   The end result of wisdom is good deeds.

- Babylonian Talmud

894.   Knowing what to do is, very different than actually doing it.

- Seth Godin

895.   High achievement always takes place in the framework of
high expectation.

- Jack and Garry Kinder

896.   Life does not happen to us. Life happens from us.

- Mike Wickett

897.   The aim of the wise is not to secure pleasure but to avoid
pain.

- Aristotle

898.   Sometimes you just have to jump and grow your wings on the way down.

- Les Brown

899.   It is better to err on the side of daring than the side of caution.

- Alvin Toffler

900.   Wishing to be friends is quick work, but friendship is a slow ripening fruit.

- Aristotle

901.   First, say to yourself what you would be; and then do what you have to do.

- Epictetus

902.   For one swallow does not make a summer and so too one day does not make a man happy.

- Aristotle

903.   When life gives you a hundred reasons to cry, show life that you have a thousand reasons to smile.

- Anon

904.   Courage is not the towering oak that sees storms come and go; it is the fragile blossom that opens in the snow.

- Alice Mackenzie Swaim

905.   **Difficulty is not an obstacle, it is an attribute.**

- **Wal Sakuluk**

906.   Your life is magnificent not because someone says it is, but because you choose to see it as such.

- Ralph Marston

907.   Integrity without knowledge is weak and useless, and knowledge without integrity is dangerous and dreadful.

- Samuel Johnson

908.   A mistake is only a mistake if you don't learn from it.

- Anon

909.   A person who graduated yesterday and stops studying today is uneducated tomorrow.

- Anon

910.   Don't let yesterday take up too much of today.

- Will Rogers

911.   The pessimist sees difficulty in opportunity; the optimist sees opportunity in every difficulty.

- Winston Churchill

912.   Coming together is a beginning; keeping together is progress; working together is success.

- Henry Ford

913.   Happiness is not a station to arrive at, but a manner of traveling.

- Margaret Lee Runbeck

914.   Your life does not get better by chance, it gets better by change.

- Jim Rohn

915.   Strive for excellence, not perfection.

- H. Jackson Brown Jr.

916.   Plan you work and work your plan.

- Napoleon Hill

917.   Make your vocation into vacation and you will not have to work a single day.

- Nicholas Lore

918.   The meeting of preparation with opportunity generates the offspring we call luck.

- Tony Robbins

919.   To conquer fear begins wisdom.

- Bertrand Russell

920.   Winners make it happen; Losers let it happen.

- Leonard Lavin

921.   To love one's self is the beginning of a lifelong romance.

- Oscar Wilde

922.   The best things in the world cannot be seen; they must be felt with the heart.

- Helen Keller

923.   True love begins when nothing is looked for in return.

- Antoine De Saint-Exupery

924.   Love must be as much a light, as it is a flame.

- Henry David Thoreau

925.   A joyful heart is the inevitable result of a heart burning with love.

- Mother Teresa

926.   The good life is inspired by love and guided by knowledge.

- Bertrand Russell

927.   We can only learn to love by loving.

- Iris Murdoch

928.   Love is a medicine for the sickness of the world; a prescription often given, too rarely taken.

- Karl Menninger

929.   Love is a canvas furnished by nature and embroidered by imagination.

- Voltaire

930.   We are all born for love. It is the principle of existence, and its only end.

- Benjamin Disreli

931.   Love until it hurts.

- Mother Teresa

932.   Men always want to be a woman's first love—women like to be a man's last romance.

- Oscar Wilde

933. Everything is clearer when you're in love.

- John Lennon

934. Love is like war; easy to begin but very hard to stop.

- Henry Louis Mencken

935. I can live without money, but I cannot live without love.

- Judy Garland

936. Sometimes the heart sees what is invisible to the eye.

- Jackson Brown Jr.

937. Courage is the first of human qualities because it is the quality which guarantees the others.

- Aristotle

938. When I saw you I fell in love. And you smiled because you knew.

- Arrigo Boito

939. A loving heart is the beginning of all knowledge.

- Thomas Carlyle

940. Love is an irresistible desire to be irresistibly desired.

- Robert Frost

941. Who, being loved, is poor?

- Oscar Wilde

942. Real love stories never have endings.

- Richard Bach

943. Some love lasts a lifetime. True love lasts forever.

- Anon

944. Plan for the future, because that is where you are going to spend the rest of your life.

- Mark Twain

945. The future is something which everyone reaches at the rate of sixty minutes an hour, whatever he does, whoever he is.

- C.S. Lewis

946.   The future is as bright as the promises of God.

- William Carey

947.   It takes courage to know when you ought to be afraid.

- James A. Michener

948.   Clear thinking requires courage rather than intelligence.

- Thomas Szasz

949.   Courage is found in unlikely places.

- J.R.R. Tolkien

950.   Courage is resistance to fear, mastery of fear, not absence of
fear.

- Mark Twain

951.   Despair gives courage to a coward.

- Thomas Fuller

952.   It takes a great deal of courage to follow another person's
lead.

- Bill Hybels

953.   The secret to happiness is freedom. The secret to freedom is
courage.

- Thucydides

954.   Honest conviction is my courage; the Constitution is my
guide.

- Andrew Johnson

955.   A man of character in peace is a man of courage in war.

- Charles Wilson

956.   Mediocrity knows nothing higher than itself, but talent
instantly recognizes genius.

- Arthur Conan Doyle

957.   Optimism is the foundation of courage.

- Nicholas M. Butler

958.   Every man of courage is a man of his word.

- Pierre Corneille

959.   Courage in danger is half the battle.
                                - Titus Maccius Plautus

960.   Necessity does the work of courage.
                                - Nicholas M. Butler

961.   Courage without conscience is a beast.
                                - Robert Green Ingersoll

962.   Without courage, wisdom bears no fruit.
                                - Baltasar Gracian

963.   Courage is grace under pressure.
                                - Ernest Hemingway

964.   The greatest test of courage on earth is to bear defeat without losing heart.
                                - Robert Green Ingersoll

965.   Courage follows action.
                                - Mack R. Douglas

966.   The past does not equal the future.
                                - Tony Robbins

967.   The future destiny of the child is always the work of the mother.
                                - Napoleon

968.   There are certain moments when we might wish the future were built by men of the past.
                                - Jean Rostand

969.   I have frequently gained my first real insight into the character of parents by studying their children.
                                - Arthur Conan Doyle

970.   Create your future from your future, not your past.
                                - Werner Erhard

971.   Cradle of the future is the grave of the past.
                                - Franz Grillparzer

972.   When men speak of the future, the Gods laugh.

- Chinese Proverb

973.   The future comes slowly, the present flies, and the past stands still forever.

- Johann Friedrich Von Schiller

974.   A real friend is one who walks in when the rest of the world walk out.

- Walter Winchell

975.   A best friend is someone who knows all about you and loves you anyway.

- Elbert Hubbard

976.   You are not very good if you are not better than your best friends imagine you to be.

- Johann Kaspar Lavater

977.   It takes a long time to grow an old friend.

- John Leonard

978.   A friend is a gift one give oneself.

- Robert Louis Stevenson

979.   My best friend is the one who brings out the best of me.

- Henry Ford

980.   A friend is someone who lets you have total freedom to be yourself.

- Jim Morrison

981.   Depend upon it there comes a time when for every addition of knowledge you forget something that you knew before. It is of the highest importance, therefore, not to have useless facts elbowing out the useful ones.

- Arthur Conan Doyle

982.   Each friend represents a world in us, a world possibly not born until they arrive.

- Anais Nin

983.   Walking with a friend in the dark is better than walking
alone in the light.

- Helen Keller

984.   It is the friends you can call up at 4 a.m. that matter.
- Marlene Dietrich

985.   Let us be grateful to people who make us happy, they are
the charming gardeners who make our souls blossom.

- Marcel Proust

986.   Hold a true friend with both your hands.
- Nigerian Proverb

987.   The most beautiful discovery true friends make is that they
can grow separately without growing apart.

- Elisabeth Foley

988.   True friendship comes when silence between two people is
comfortable.

- Dave Tyson Gentry

989.   Discretion is the greatest part of valor.
- English Proverb

990.   What we call Man's power over Nature turns out to be a
power exercise by some men over other men with Nature as its
instrument.

- Anon

991.   A true friend is one who overlooks your failures and
tolerates your success.

- Doug Larson

992.   Friends are relatives you make for yourself.
- Eustache Deschamps

993.   No road is long with good company.
- Turkish Proverb

994.   The squeaky wheel gets the grease.
- English Proverb

995. My dream concept is that I have a camera and I am trying to
      photograph what is essentially invisible. And every once in a while
      I get a glimpse of her and I grab the picture.

                                            - Leonard Nimoy

996. For strange effects and extraordinary combinations we must go
      to life itself, which is always far more daring than any effort of the
      imagination.

                                            - Arthur Conan Doyle

997. A thing of beauty is a joy forever.

                                            - English Proverb

998. A friend is known when needed.

                                            - Saudi Proverb

999. Beauty without virtue is like a rose without scent.

                                            - Swedish Proverb

1000. A bit of fragrance always clings to the hand that gives roses.
                                            - Chinese Proverb

1001. It is not for the swan to teach eaglets to sing.

                                            - Danish Proverb

1002. Experience this moment to its fullest.

                                            - Zen Proverb

1003. Friendship doubles our joy and divides our grief.
                                            - Swedish Proverb

1004. If you want a friend, be a friend.

                                            - English Proverb

1005. One must learn to make others happy if one wants to be happy.
                                            - Swedish Proverb

1006. The eye never forgets what the heart has seen.
                                            - African Proverb

1007. He who envies others does not obtain peace of mind.
                                            - Zen Proverb

1008. Music in the soul can be heard by the universe.
- Taoist Proverb

1009. Gardens are not made by sitting in the shade.
- English Proverb

1010. A child is what you put into him.
- African Proverb

1011. It is no use to wait for your ship to come in unless you have sent one out.
- Belgian Proverb

1012. He who knows how to live, knows enough.
- Spanish Proverb

1013. What you think you are, you are, until you think otherwise.
- American Proverb

1014. A fable is a bridge which leads to the truth. Follow it.
- Saudi Proverb

1015. The true artist perseveres no matter what the critics say.
- Dutch Proverb

1016. You already possess everything necessary to become great.
- Native American Proverb

1017. The obstacle is the path.
- Zen Proverb

1018. To be calm is the highest achievement of the self.
- Zen Proverb

1019. A friend's frown is better than a fool's smile.
- English Proverb

1020. Anyone who sees beauty and does not look at it will soon be poor.
- Yoruban Proverb

1021. Be not afraid of going slowly, be afraid of standing still.

- Chinese Proverb

1022. A friend in need is a friend indeed.

- American Proverb

1023. A friend is easier lost than found.

- Anon

1024. A problem shared is a problem halved.

- English Proverb

1025. A true friend is someone who reaches for your hand, but touches your heart.

- Anon

1026. A man should keep his little brain attic stocked with all the furniture that he is likely to use, and the rest he can put away in the lumber room of his library, where he can get it if he wants.

- Arthur Conan Doyle

1027. False friends are worse than open enemies.

- Zen Proverb

1028. Flattery is alright so long as you don't inhale.

- Anon

1029. The best things are not bought and sold.

- American Proverb

1030. A loveless life is a living death.

- Anon

1031. Hatred is as blind as love.

- Anon

1032. Love and a cough cannot be hid.

- Anon

1033. Love levels all inequalities.

- Anon

1034.   Love sought is good, but given unsought is better.

- Anon

1035.   The course of love never did run smooth.

- Anon

1036.   He that hurts another, hurts himself.

- Anon

1037.   Heavy givers are light complainers.

- Anon

1038.   If you lose your temper, don't look for it.

- Zen Proverb

1039.   Never let the sun set on angry heart.

- Zen Proverb

1040.   Temper is so good a thing that we should never lose it.

- Zen Proverb

1041.   To the world you may be one person, but to one person, you may be the world.

- Buddhist Proverb

1042.   A bully is always a coward.

- Anon

1043.   A good thing is all the sweeter when won with pain.

- Anon

1044.   As you go through life, make this your goal, watch the doughnut and not the hole.

- Anon

1045.   Leave tomorrow for tomorrow.

- Zen Proverb

1046.   No man is worse for knowing the worst of himself.

- Anon

1047.   Procrastination is the thief of time.

- English Proverb

1048. Experience is the hardest teacher. She gives the test first and the lesson afterwards.

- Anon

1049. Better late thrive than never do well.

- English Proverb

1050. If you don't say it you will not have to unsay it.

- Buddhist Proverb

1051. Silence is an excellent remedy against slander.

- Anon

1052. Speak clearly, if you speak at all.

- Zen Proverb

1053. A change is as good as rest.

- Anon

1054. A wise man shall hold his tongue till he sees his opportunity.

- Anon

1055. It is better to stay silent and be thought a fool, than to open one's mouth and remove all doubt.

- Anon

1056. No one can be caught in places he does not visit.

- American Proverb

1057. No wise man ever wishes to be younger.

- Buddhist Proverb

1058. Where observation is concerned, chance favors only the prepared mind.

- Anon

1059. Wisdom is neither inheritance nor a legacy.

- Anon

1060. A man too careful of danger lives in continual torment.

- Buddhist Proverb

1061. Don't try kicking against the wind.

- Anon

1062. If you can't help, don't hinder.

- Anon

1063. To the man who loves art for its own sake, it is frequently in its least important and lowliest manifestations that the keenest pleasure is to be derived.

- Arthur Conan Doyle

1064. Maybe all one can do is hope to end up with the right regrets.

- Arthur Miller

1065. If you see something you like, take it and make it better.

- Anon

1066. It is easy to criticize others work, when you are not working.

- Anon

1067. Not to break is better than to mend.

- Anon

1068. It is no use closing the stable door, after the horse has bolted.

- Anon

1069. Affairs are easier of entrance than of exit; and it is but common prudence to see our way out before we venture in.

- Aesop

1070. A groom spent long hours combing and clipping the horse he charged but daily stole a portion of his oats to sell for profit.
The horse got into a bad condition and at last cried,
"If you want me to look sleek and well, you must comb me less and feed me more."

- Aesop

1071. Have I played the part well?
Then applaud as I exit.

- Augustus, last words of the first Roman Emperor

1072. You get what you want in life, but not your second choice too.

- Alison Lurie

1073. Letting the cat out of the cat is a lot easier than putting it back in.

- Will Rogers

1074. Evil is whatever distracts.

- Franz Kafka

1075. An appeaser is one who feeds a crocodile – hoping it will feed him last.

- Winston Churchill

1076. Now I am become Death, the destroyer of worlds.
- J. Robert Oppenheimer
(father of the atomic bomb) upon witnessing the first tests

1077. A hen is heavy when carried far.

- Irish Proverb

1078. The one who loves the least, controls the relationship.
- Robert Anthony

1079. A hound's food is in its legs.

- Irish Proverb

1080. Anyone who cannot come to terms with his life while he is alive needs one hand to ward off a little his despair over his fate… but with his other hand, he can note down what he sees among the ruins.

- Franz Kafka

1081. There comes a time when you have to stop crossing oceans for people who won't even jump a puddle for you.

- Anon

1082. A man is not honest simply because he never had a chance to steal.

- Yiddish Proverb

1083. A man should live if only to satisfy his curiosity.

- Yiddish Proverb

1084. Men deal with life, as children with their play
Who first misuse, then cast their toys away.

        - William Cowper

1085. A man may well bring a horse to the water, but he cannot make him drink.

        - John Heywood

1086. Most people are other people.
Their thoughts are someone else's opinions, their lives a mimicry, their passions a quotation.

        - Oscar Wilde

1087. Believing in progress does not mean believing that any progress is made.

        - Franz Kafka

1088. The theatre is so endlessly fascinating because it's so accidental. It's so much like life.

        - Arthur Miller

1089. The brain is wider than the sky.

        - Emily Dickinson

1090. It's not whether you get knocked down, it's whether you get up.
        - Vince Lombardi

1091. A new broom sweeps clean, but the old brush knows all the corners.

        - Irish Proverb

1092. A rumor goes in one ear and out many mouths.
        - Chinese Proverb

1093. A society grows great when old men plant trees whose shade they known they shall never sit in.

        - Greek Proverb

1094. If a man with experience meets a man with money, the experienced man gets the money and the formally rich man gets an experience.

        - Anon

1095. A silent mouth is melodious.

- Irish Proverb

1096. Success is a lousy teacher. It seduces smart people into thinking they can't lose.

- Bill Gates

1097. I don't believe in astrology; I'm a Sagittarius, and we're skeptical.

- Arthur C. Clarke

1098. Behind every argument is someone's ignorance.

- Robert Benchley

1099. A perfect relationship isn't ever actually perfect, it's just one where both people never give up.

- Anon

1100. A soft answer turneth away wrath: but grievous words stir up anger.

- Bible - Proverbs 15:1

1101. A spoon does not know the taste of soup, nor a learned fool the taste of wisdom.

- Welsh Proverb

1102. You can fool some of the people all of the time, you can fool all of the people some of the time but you can never fool all of the people all of the time.

- Abraham Lincoln

1103. Happiness is a by-product, not a goal.

- Eleanor Roosevelt

1104. Never befriend one who's not better than thyself.

- Confucius

1105. You can't move so fast that you try to change the mores faster than people can accept it. That doesn't mean you do nothing, but it means that you do the things that need to be done according to the priority.

- Eleanor Roosevelt

1106. A son is a son till he gets him a wife,
But a daughter's a daughter the rest of your life.

- Anon

1107. Anger is never without an argument, but seldom with a good one.

- Indira Gandhi

1108. A thief believes everybody steals.

- Anon

1109. A thorn defends the rose, harming those who would steal the blossom.

- Chinese Proverb

1110. Cleverness is not wisdom.

- Euripides

1111. The hardest thing in the world to understand is income taxes.

- Albert Einstein

1112. The universe is under no obligation to make sense to you.

- Neil de Grasse Tyson

1113. The best of seers is he who guesses well.

- Euripides

1114. Nothing contributes so much to tranquilize the mind as a steady purpose - a point on which the soul may fix its intellectual eye.

- Mary Shelley

1115. When you dance, your purpose is not to get to a certain place on the floor. It's to enjoy each step along the way.

- Wayne Dyer

1116. I do not wish women to have power over men; but over themselves.

- Mary Shelley

1117. Happiness is brief. God batters its sails.

- Euripides

1118. A throne is only a bench covered in velvet.

- French Proverb

1119. There are mysteries which men can only guess at, which age by age they may solve only in part.

- Bram Stoker

1120. Technology is just a tool. In terms of getting the kids working together and motivating them, the teacher is the most important.

- Bill Gates

1121. If you change the way you look at things, the things you look at change.

- Wayne Dyer

1122. Fashion is a form of ugliness so intolerable, we have to update it every six months.

- Oscar Wilde

1123. A tree falls the way it leans.

- Bulgarian Proverb

1124. If you can't make it good, at least make it look good.

- Bill Gates

1125. Only three types of people tell the truth; kids, drunk people and anyone who is really really angry.

- Richard Pryor

1126. He who lives by the sword, dies by the sword.

- Jesus Christ

1127. My life is my message.

- Mahatma Gandhi

1128. Invention, it must be humbly admitted, does not consist in creating out of void, but out of chaos.

- Mary Shelley

1129. If a writer knows enough about what he is writing about, he may omit things that he knows. The dignity of movement of an iceberg is due to only one ninth of it being above water

- Ernest Hemingway

1130. To love beauty is to see light.

- Victor Hugo

1131. We humans have millions of years of evolutionary baggage that makes us regard competition in a deadly light.

- Vernor Vinge

1132. A wise man hears one word and understands two.

- Yiddish Proverb

1133. Nobody wants to hear this, but sometimes the person you want most is the person you're best without.

- Anon

1134. My dreams were all my own; I accounted for them to nobody; they were my refuge when annoyed – my dearest pleasure when free.

- Mary Shelley

1135. He is rich who rejoices in his portion.

- Benjamin Franklin

1136. A wise man makes his own decisions, an ignorant man follows the public opinion.

- Chinese Proverb

1137. A man who does not trust himself will never really trust anybody.

- Jean-Francois Paul de Gondi, Cardinal de Retz (Memoires)

1138. Politeness has become so rare that some people mistake it for flirtation.

- Anon

1139. Being ignorant is not so much a shame, as being unwilling to learn.

- Benjamin Franklin

1140. A worth woman is far more precious than jewels; strength and dignity are her clothing.

- Bible – Proverbs 31

1141. Advice should be viewed from behind.

- Swedish Proverb

1142. If you reveal your secrets to the wind, you should blame the wind for revealing them to the trees.

- Khali Gibran

1143. Act in the valley so that you need not fear those who stand on the hill.

- Danish Proverb

1144. And those who were seen dancing were thought to be insane by those who could not hear the music.

- Friedrich Nietzsche

1145. The apple cannot be stuck back on the Tree of Knowledge; once we begin to see, we are doomed and challenged to seek the strength to see more, not less.

- Arthur Miller

1146. By all means let's be open-minded, but not so open-minded that our brains drop out.

- Richard Dawkins

1147. I've always been more comfortable sinking while clutching a good theory than swimming with an ugly fact.

- David Mamet

1148. Education is learning what you didn't even know you didn't know.

- Daniel J. Boorstin

1149. All things grow with time, except grief.

- Yiddish Proverb

1150. We are at our most destructive when we think we are indestructible.

- Mike Fisher

1151. No man ever believes that the Bible means what it says; he is always convinced that it says what he means.

- George Bernard Shaw

1152. There is no rule on how to write. Sometimes it comes easily and perfectly; sometimes its like drilling rock and then blasting it out with charges.

- Ernest Hemingway

1153. We do not see things as they are, we see things as we are.

- Anon

1154. Attraction is beyond our will or ideas sometimes.

- Juliette Binoche

1155. A dream is what makes people love life even when it is painful.

- Theodore Zeldin

1156. An angry man is not fit to pray.

- Yiddish Proverb

1157. An enemy will agree, but a friend will argue.

- Russian Proverb

1158. Don't be seduced into thinking that which does not make a profit is without value.

- Arthur Miller

1159. But O, how bitter a thing it is to look into happiness through another man's eyes.

- William Shakespeare

1160. Don't burn your bed to catch a flea.

- Turkish Proverb

1161. An old rat is a brave rat.

- French Proverb

1162. Anger can be an expensive luxury.

- Italian Proverb

1163. I do sometimes accuse people of ignorance, but that is not intended to be an insult. I'm ignorant of lots of things. Ignorance is sometimes what can be remedied by education.

- Richard Dawkins

1164. When you judge another, you do not define them, you define yourself.

- Wayne Dyer

1165. Each person is an enigma. You're a puzzle not only to yourself but also to everyone else, and the great mystery of our time is how we penetrate this puzzle.

- Theodore Zeldin

1166. People will question all the good things they hear about you but believe all the bad without a second thought.

- Anon

1167. Falling in love is not at all the most stupid thing that people do but gravitation cannot be held responsible for it.

- Albert Einstein

1168. Haste is blind.

- Titus Livius

1169. We should strive to be employed in such a way that we don't realize that what we're doing is work.

- Theodore Zeldin

1170. People who want the most approval get the least.

- Wayne Dyer

1171. To idolize a person means you don't get to know them, and the idea that you can become one is a myth, and it also means that you don't need to talk to one another because you're the same person.

- Theodore Zeldin

1172. Isn't it a remarkable coincidence almost everyone has the same religion as their parents? And it always just happens to be the right religion. Religions run in families. If we'd been brought up in ancient Greece, we would all be worshipping Zeus and Apollo. If we had been born Vikings, we would be worshipping Wotan and Thor. How does come about? Through childhood indoctrination.

- Richard Dawkins

1173. He who displays himself does not shine. He who stands on his toes does not stand well.

- Chinese Proverb

1174. A wise girl kisses but doesn't love, listens but doesn't believe, and leaves before she is left.

- Marilyn Monroe

1175. No man is justified in doing evil on the ground of expedience.

- Theodore Roosevelt

1176. The closer a man approaches tragedy the more intense is his concentration of emotion upon the fixed point of his commitment, which is to say the closer he approaches what in life we can fanaticism.

- Arthur Miller

1177. Anger is as a stone cast into a wasp's nest.

- Malabr Proverb

1178. A thing of beauty is a joy forever, its loveliness increases, it will never pass into nothingness.

- John Keats

1179. I used to think that the worst thing in life was to end up all alone. It's not. The worst thing in life is ending up with people who make you feel alone.

- Robin Williams

1180. The components of anxiety, stress, fear and anger do not exist independently of you in the world. They simply do not exist in the physical world, even though we talk about them as if they do.

- Wayne Dyer

1181. And it seems to me important for a country, for a nation to certainly know about its glorious achievements but also to know where its ideals failed, in order to keep that from happening again.

- George Takei

1182. If a child can't learn the way we teach, maybe we should teach the way we learn.

- Michael J. Fox

1183. The one who boasts will only gain one thing: enemies.

- Anon

1184. He who vaunts himself does not find his merit acknowledged.

– Chinese Proverb

1185. Your most unhappy customers are your greatest source of learning.

- Bill Gates

1186. If science proves some belief of Buddhism wrong, then Buddhism will have to change.

- Dalai Lama

1187. You have brains in your head.
    You have feet in your shoes.
    You can steer yourself in any direction you choose.
    You're on your own, and you know what you know.
    And you are the guy who'll decide where to go.

- Dr. Seuss

1188. Whom the gods wish to destroy they first call promising.

– Cyril Connolly
(Enemies of Promise)

1189. Just because you're offended, doesn't mean you're right.

- Ricky Gervais

1190. Every hero becomes a bore at last.

– Ralph Emerson

1191. I don't care what you think about me, I don't think about you at all.

- Jack Nicholson

1192. People ask you for criticism, but they only want praise.

– W. Somerset Maugham

1193. Change will not come if we wait for some other person or some other time. We are the ones we've been waiting for. We are the change that we seek.

- Barack Obama

1194. As a dog returneth to his vomit, so a fool returneth to his folly.

- Bible - Proverbs 26:11

1195. Don't cry because it's over. Smile because it happened.

- Dr. Seuss

1196. I've always tried to go a step past wherever people expected me to end up.

- Beverly Sills

1197. Normal is getting dressed in clothes that you buy for work and driving through traffic in a car that you are still paying for – in order to get to the job you need to pay for the clothes and the car, and the house you leave vacant all day so you can afford to live in it.

- Ellen Goodman

1198. As a man thinketh in his heart, so is he.

- Bible – Proverbs 23:7

1199. Compliments cost nothing, yet many pay dear for them.

- Thomas Fuller

1200. If you can't explain it simply, you don't understand it well enough.

- Albert Einstein

1201. Always write angry letters to your enemies. Never mail them.

- James Fallows

1202. Destiny can justify a tyrant's authority for crime or a fool's excuse for failure.

- Ambrose Bierce

1203. Respect your parents. They passed school without Google.

- Anon

1204. Climb mountains to see lowlands.

- Chinese Proverb

1205. Darkness reigns at the foot of the lighthouse.

- Japanese Proverb

1206. I not only use all the brains that I have, but all that I can borrow.

- Woodrow Wilson

1207. The more you praise and celebrate your life, the more there is in life to celebrate.

- Oprah Winfrey

1208. The more that you read, the more things you will know. The more that you learn, the more places you'll go.

- Dr. Seuss

1209. In the last few years, the very idea of telling the truth, the whole truth, and nothing but the truth is dredged up only as a final resort when the alternative options of deception, threat and bribery have all been exhausted.

- Michael Musto

1210. Failure is another stepping stone to greatness.

- Oprah Winfrey

1211. Deal with the faults of others as gently as with your own.

- Chinese Proverb

1212. Children are poor men's riches.

- English Proverb

1213. Sometimes legends make reality, and become more useful than the facts.

- Salman Rushdie

1214. Surround yourself with only people who are going to lift you higher.

- Oprah Winfrey

1215. As cold waters to a thirsty soul, so is good news from a far country.

- Bible – Proverbs 25:25

1216. He has all the virtues I dislike and none of the vices I admire.

- Winston Churchill

1217. He who permits himself to tell a lie once, finds it much easier to do it a second and a third time till at length it becomes habitual.

- Thomas Jefferson

1218. Everyone wants to be successful until they see what it actually takes.

- Anon

1219. Better give a penny then lend twenty.

- Italian Proverb

1220. I like nonsense, it wakes up the brain cells. Fantasy is a necessary ingredient in living, it's a way of looking at life through the wrong end of a telescope. Which is what I do, and that enables you to laugh at life's realities.

- Dr. Seuss

1221. You get fat if you take in more calories than you burn. That's simple science. Everybody knows this. It doesn't sneaky up on you. It's a fact.

-Ricky Gervais

1222. A people free to choose will always choose peace.

- Ronald Reagan

1223. Death always comes too early or too late.

- English Proverb

1224. If a single teacher can't teach all the subjects, then how can you expect a single student to learn all subjects?

- Anon

1225. It is less shameful for a king to be overcome by force of arms than by bribery.

- Sallust

1226. I don't understand why people think that having a gay child means they failed as a parent. Disowning your child means you failed as a parent.

- Anon

1227. Death closes all doors.

- English Proverb

1228. Do not look where you fell but where you slipped.

- African Proverb

1229. Do not rejoice at my grief, for when mine is old, yours will be new.

- Spanish Proverb

1230. You have a choice - you either joined or formed a gang or you let others bully you.

- Jack Bowman

1231. Do not talk Arabic in the house of a Moor.

- Oriental Proverb

1232. Yes, evolution is a theory. Gravity is just a theory too. Anyone who doubts it is welcome to jump out of a ten story window.

- Richard Dawkins

1233. You can discover what your enemy fears most by observing the means he uses to frighten you.

- Eric Hoffer

1234. A bee is never as busy as it seems; it's just that it can't buzz any slower.

- Kin Hubbard

1235. Normal is an illusion. What is normal for the spider is chaos for the fly.

- Morticia Addams
(The Addams Family)

1236. It can't be something that you're doing to lose weight, and then once you do, you're done. I do it every day of my life.

- LeAnn Rimes

1237. You'd never invite a thief into your house. So why would you allow thoughts that steal your joy to makes themselves at home in your mind?

- Anon

1238. True reconciliation does not consist in merely forgetting the past.

- Nelson Mandela

1239. Death pays all debts.

- English Proverb

1240. No weapon has ever settled a moral problem. It can impose a solution but it cannot guarantee it to be a just one.

- Ernest Hemingway

1241. Those who don't study history are doomed to repeat it. Yet those who study history are doomed to stand by helplessly while everyone else repeats it.

- Anon

1242. For me context is the key - from that comes the understanding of everything.

- Kenneth Noland

1243. If you think adventure is dangerous, try routine, it's lethal.

- Paulo Coelho

1244. It seems to me that everything that happens to us is a disconcerting mix of choice and contingency.

- Penelope Lively

1245. We all have that one friend who always gives relationship advice but is still single.

- Anon

1246. The components to power are those who-
Want it, Give it, Control it.

- Anon

1247. The strength of the pack is the wolf, and strength of the wolf is the pack.

– Rudyard Kipling

1248. All the war-propaganda, all the screaming and lies and hatred, comes invariably from people who are not fighting.

- George Orwell

1249. The opposite of talking should be listening, not waiting.

- Anon

1250. It's never your successful friends posting the inspirational quotes.

- Damien Fahey

1251. It is the province of knowledge to speak and it is the privilege of wisdom to listen.

- Oliver Wendell Holmes

1252. Holding a grudge is letting someone live rent-free in your head.

- Anon

1253. The world is an oyster, but you don't crack it open on a mattress.

– Arthur Miller

1254. Do not speak of secrets in a field that is full of little hills.

- Hebrew Proverb

1255. The best sign of a healthy relationship is no sign of it online.

- Anon

1256. Tell me what you eat, and I will tell you what you are.

- Anon

1257. Do not use a hatchet to remove a fly from your friend's forehead.

- Chinese Proverb

1258. All books are divisible into two classes, the books of the hour, and the books of all time.

- John Ruskin

1259. Hesitation increases in relation to risk in equal proportion to age.
- Ernest Hemingway

1260. Cooking is the most ancient of the arts, for Adam was born hungry.

– Anthelme Brillat-Savarin
(The Physiology of Taste)

1261. Don't imitate the fly before you have wings.

- French Proverb

1262. If one does not know to which port is sailing, no wind is favorable.

- Lucius Annaeus Seneca

1263. Even a small thorn causes festering.

- Irish Proverb

1264. Everyone is kneaded out of the same dough but not baked in the same oven.

- Yiddish Proverb

1265. Never think that war, no matter how necessary, nor how justified, is not a crime.

- Ernest Hemingway

1266. He that gives good advice, builds with one hand; he that gives good counsel and example, build with both; but he that gives good admonition and bad example, builds with one hand and pulls down with the other.

- Francis Bacon

1267. Most people return great favors with one thing – ingratitude.

- Benjamin Franklin

1268. God created war so that Americans would learn geography.

- Mark Twain

1269. Nothing gives one person so much advantage over another as to remain always cool and unruffled under all circumstances.

- Thomas Jefferson

1270. If you're not careful, the newspapers will have you hating the people who are being oppressed, and loving the people who are doing the oppressing.

- Malcolm Little

1271. Celebrities who have plastic surgery don't look younger or more attractive. They just look like people who had plastic surgery.

– Kate Winslet

1272. Everyone loves justice in the affairs of another.

- Italian Proverb

1273. I always wondered why somebody didn't do something about that, then I realized I am somebody.

- Anon

1274. Everyone pushes a falling fence.

- Chinese Proverb

1275. Experience is a comb which nature gives to men when they are bald.

- Eastern Proverb

1276. I don't need the fillers and additives to taint the natural goodness of real food.

- Mark Hyman

1277. Credit goes to the man who convinces the world, not the man whom the idea first occurs.

- Franic Darwin

1278. Tell me and I forget. Teach me and I remember. Involve me and I learn.

- Benjamin Franklin

1279. I love rumors. I always find out amazing things about myself I never knew.

- Anon

1280. A prudent question is one-half of wisdom.

- Francis Bacon

1281. Not knowing when the dawn will come, I open ever door.

- Emily Dickinson

1282. It's amazing what you can accomplish if you don't care who gets the credit.

- Harry Truman

1283. By imposing too great a responsibility or rather all of it, you crush yourself.

- Franz Kafka

1284. A word is dead when it is said, some say. I say it just begins to live that day.

- Emily Dickinson

1285. Silence can be the worst criticism.

- Charles Buxton

1286. Someone needs to explain to me why wanting clean drinking water makes you an activist, and why proposing to destroy water with chemical warfare doesn't make a corporation a terrorist.

- Winona Laduke

1287. When you gradually add in nutrient-dense, fiber-rich foods, you simply stop feeling cravings. Instead of craving, you feel full, fulfilled, and content.

- Kathy Freston

1288. I don't know how people can fake whole relationships. I can't even fake a hello to somebody I don't like.

- Anon

1289. If your parents didn't leave you when you were young, then don't leave them when they are old.

- Anon

1290. The trouble with having an open mind, of course, is that people will insist on coming along and trying to put things in it.

- Terry Pratchett

1291. Proximity to power deludes some into thinking they wield it.
- Frank Underwood
(House of Cards)

1292. Don't despair, not even over the fact that you don't despair.
- Franz Kafka

1293. Damaged people are the most dangerous kind, because they already know they can survive.

- Anon

1294. In 100 or 200 years' time, we may look back on the way we treat animals today as something like we today look back on the way our forefathers treated slaves.

- Richard Dawkins

1295. I learned never to empty the well of my writing, but always to stop when there was still something there in the deep part of the well, and let it refill at night from the springs that fed it.

- Ernest Hemingway

1296. We should feel sorrow, but not sink under its oppression.

- Confucius

1297. The superior man acts before he speaks, and afterwards speaks according to his action.

- Kong Qiu

1298. The superior man understands what is right; the inferior man understands what will sell.

- Chinese Proverb

1299. As far as eating is concerned, humans are the most stupid animals on the planet. We kill billions of wild animals to protect the animals that we eat. We are destroying our environment to feed to the animals we eat. We spend more time, money and resources fattening up the animals that we eat, than we do feeding humans who are dying of hunger. The greatest irony is that after all the expense of raising these animals, we eat them; and they kill us slowly. And rather than recognize this madness, we torture and murder millions of other animals trying to find cures to disease caused by eating animals in the first place.

- Mike Anderson

1300. Earth provides enough to satisfy every man's needs, but not every man's greed.

- Mahatma Gandhi

1301. Hatred is self-punishment.

- Hosea Ballou

1302. There is no friend as loyal as a book.

- Ernest Hemingway

1303. When you cease to make a contribution, you begin to die.

- Eleanor Roosevelt

1304. The superior man is modest in his speech, but exceeds in his actions.

- Confucius

1305. The cruelest lies are told in silence.

- Adlai Stevenson

1306. The best propaganda is more propaganda.

- Edward Bernays

1307. An oppressive government is more to be feared than a tiger.

- Confucius

1308. My experience has been that work is almost the best way to pull oneself out of the depths.

- Eleanor Roosevelt

1309. If I read a book and it makes my whole body so cold, no fire can ever warm me, I know that is poetry.

- Emily Dickinson

1310. If all insects on Earth disappeared, within 50 years all life on Earth would end. If human beings disappeared from the Earth, within 50 years all forms of life would flourish.

- Jonas Salk

1311. To be wronged is nothing unless you continue to remember it.

- Kong Qiu

1312. You can get help from teachers, but you are going to have to learn a lot by yourself, sitting alone in a room.

- Dr. Seuss

1313. Be thankful for what you have; you'll end up having more. If you concentrate on what you don't have, you will never, ever have enough.

- Oprah Winfrey

1314. Fortune is a woman: if you neglect her today do not expect to regain her tomorrow.

- French Proverb

1315. Flattery makes friends and truth makes enemies.

- Spanish Proverb

1316. How few there are who have courage enough to own their faults, or resolution enough to mend them.

- Benjamin Franklin

1317. Good wine ruins the purse, and bad wine ruins the stomach.
- English Proverb

1318. Everything you are against weakens you. Everything you are for empowers you.
- Wayne Dyer

1319. Never before have humans been so ambitious, have they thought that they could be much more than their parents were.
- Theodore Zeldin

1320. I don't think of myself as a poor deprived ghetto girl who made good. I think of myself as somebody who from an early age knew I was responsible for myself and I had to make good.
- Oprah Winfrey

1321. We are all born ignorant, but one must work hard to remain stupid.
- Benjamin Franklin

1322. Greediness burst the bag.
- American Proverb

1323. Grumbling makes the loaf no larger.
- English Proverb

1324. Half a loaf is better than none.
- English Proverb

1325. Where there is no struggle, there is no strength.
- Oprah Winfrey

1326. It's not how much we have, but how much we enjoy.
- Charles Spurgeon

1327. What can't be cured must be endured.
- English Proverb

1328. Better to be poor and healthy rather than rich and sick.
- American Proverb

1329. To be nameless in worthy deeds exceeds an infamous history.
- Sir Thomas Browne

1330. A savage is not the one who lives in the forest, but the one who destroys it.

- Anon

1331. A critic is a bundle of biases held loosely together by a sense of taste.

- Whitney Balliett

1332. The most dangerous untruths are truths moderately distorted.
- George Christoph Lichtenberg

1333. Critics, like eunuchs know how it works but they can't do it themselves.

- Anon

1334. Cruelty, like every other vice, requires no motive outside of itself; it only requires opportunity.

- George Eliot

1335. Are all men in disguise except those crying?

- Dannie Abse

1336. Cruelty would be delicious if one could only find some sort of cruelty that didn't really hurt.

- George Bernard Shaw

1337. The first voice which I uttered was crying, as all others do.
- Solomon Ibn Gabirol

1338. A good metaphor can make any idea look good.

- Scott Adams

1339. The garden is beautiful without filling it with fairies.

- William Occam

1340. Depression is frozen anger.

- Sigmund Freud

1341. A friend to all is a friend to none.

- Aristotle

1342. Beauty is a short-lived tyranny.

- Socrates

1343. Without forgiveness, life is governed... an endless cycle of resentment and retaliation.

- Roberto Assagioli

1344. To be angry with the right person and to the right degree and at the right time and for the right purpose, and in the right way – that is not easy.

- Aristotle

1345. The pleasures arising from thinking and learning will make us think and learn all the more.

- Aristotle

1346. It is not part of true culture to tame tigers, any more than it is to make sheep ferocious.

- Henry David Thoreau

1347. A people without the knowledge of their past history, origin and culture is like a tree without roots.

- Marcus Garvey

1348. Worry is a cycle of inefficient thoughts whirling around a center of fear.

- Corrie Ten Boom

1349. It is better to risk saving a guilty man than to condemn an innocent one.

- Voltaire

1350. Any fool can criticize, condemn and complain – and most fools do.

- Benjamin Franklin

1351. Love is like a friendship caught on fire. In the beginning a flame, very pretty, often hot and flickering. As love grows older, our hearts mature and our love becomes as coals, deep-burning and unquenchable.

- Bruce Lee

1352. Fortune is blind, but not invisible.

- French Proverb

1353. Dying is nothing. So start by living. It's less fun and it lasts longer.

- Romeo et Jeanette

1354. Condemn none: if you can stretch out a helping hand, do so. If you cannot, fold your hands, bless your brothers, and let them go their own way.

- Swami Vivekananda

1355. The end of man is an action and not a thought, though it were the noblest.

– Thomas Carlyle

1356. Finite to fail, but infinite to venture.

- Emily Dickinson

1357. Beware of little expenses. A small leak will sink a great ship.

- Benjamin Franklin

1358. A likely impossibility is always preferable to an unconvincing possibility.

- Aristotle

1359. There is no worse lie than a truth misunderstood by those who hear it.

- William James

1360. Doing the best at this moment puts you in the best place for the next moment.

- Oprah Winfrey

1361. The unhappy derive comfort from the misfortune of others.

- Aesop

1362. It has become appallingly obvious that our technology has exceeded our humanity.

- Albert Einstein

1363. I don't like that man. I must know him.

- Abraham Lincoln

1364. You can't choose up sides on a round world.

- Wayne Dyer

1365. Lies take more energy and yet they are easier and more common that the truth.

- J. Michael Straczynski

1366. Successful people make money. It's not that people who make money become successful, but that successful people attract money. They bring success to what they do.

- Wayne Dyer

1367. My fate cannot be mastered it can only be collaborated with and thereby, to some extent, directed. Nor am I the captain of my soul; I am only its noisiest passenger.

- Anon

1368. Dependency is death to initiative, to risk-taking and opportunity. It's time to stop the spread of dependency and fight it like the poison it is.

- Mitt Romney

1369. We have broken the cycle of dependency. People have found out they're better off working.

- John Engler

1370. One is never as unhappy as one thinks, nor as happy as one hopes.

– Dud de la Rochefoucauld

1371. That's the great paradox of living on this earth, that in the midst of great pain you can have great joy as well. If we didn't have those things we'd just be numb.

- Kathy Matthea

1372. My great concern is not whether you have failed, but whether you are content with your failure.

- Abraham Lincoln

1373. He that is discontented in one place will seldom be happy in another.

- Aesop

1374. Saying nothing sometimes says the most.

- Emily Dickinson

1375. The only thing worse than your heart breaking is your heart hardening.

- Anon

1376. The fact that you can love something that you've lost is all the incentive you need to love again, as opposed to becoming comfortably numb.

- Cee Lo Green

1377. One man that has a mind and knows it can always beat ten men who haven't and don't.

– George Bernard Shaw

1378. As far as we can discern, the sole purpose of human existence is to kindle a light of meaning in the darkness of mere being.

– C.G. Jung
(Memories, Dreams, Reflection)

1379. All good books have one thing in common – they are truer than if they had really happened.

- Ernest Hemingway

1380. If life were predictable, it would cease to be life, and be without flavor.

- Eleanor Roosevelt

1381. Few people are capable of expressing with equanimity opinions which differ from the prejudices of their social environment. Most people are even incapable of forming such opinions.

- Albert Einstein

1382. Success is counted sweetest by those who never succeed.

- Emily Dickinson

1383. We were created to create ourselves.

- Anon

1384. Ability will never catch up with the demand for it.

- Chinese Proverb

1385. To see the right and not to do it is cowardice.

- Kong Qiu

1386. You can never really live anyone else's life, not even your child's. The influence you exert is through your own life, and what you've become yourself.

- Eleanor Roosevelt

1387. It is more shameful to distrust our friends than to be deceived by them.

- Confucius

1388. Free will and destiny are two different paths that will hopefully meet each other at the end of a long road.

- Anon

1389. Coincidence is the word we use when we can't see the levers and pulleys.

- Emma Bull

1390. Most cancer-related deaths can be prevented through simple and painless preventive measures. A late diagnosis can result in more serious, long-term consequences.

- Olympia Snowe

1391. The power of intuitive understanding will protect you from harm.

- Lao Tzu

1392. Friends are like fiddle strings, they must not be screwed too tight.

- English Proverb

1393. I wonder if Americans aren't fooled by our accent into detecting brilliance that may not really be there.

- Stephen Fry

1394. Friends are lost by calling often and calling seldom.

- French Proverb

1395. Friendship is a furrow in the sand.

- Tongan Proverb

1396. Give no counsel till you are asked for it.

- Italian Proverb

1397. A man's errors are his portals of discovery.

- James Joyce

1398. I learned to change my accent; in England, your accent identifies you very strongly with a class, and I did not want to be held back.

- Sting

1399. Look at the means which a man employs, consider his motives, observe his pleasures. A man simply cannot conceal himself.

- Confucius

1400. Just because a path isn't well lit does not mean it cannot be walked on.

- Anon

1401. Two things motivate people to achieve success: inspiration and desperation.

- Anon

1402. You can have all the facts and be wrong.

- Anon

1403. If I shall exist eternally, how shall I exist tomorrow?

- Franz Kafka

1404. Discovery consists of seeing what everybody has seen and thinking what nobody has thought.

– Albert von Szent-Gyorgyi

1405. As you get older it is harder to have heroes, but it is sort of necessary.

- Ernest Hemingway

1406. A great empire, like a great cake, is most easily diminished at the edges.

- Benjamin Franklin

1407. Mediocre minds usually dismiss anything which reaches beyond their own understanding.

- Francoise de La Rochefoucauld

1408. It is better to be the hammer than the anvil.

- Emily Dickinson

1409. If matters of truth and justice, there is no difference between large and small problems, for issues concerning the treatment of people are all the same.

- Albert Einstein

1410. You shouldn't believe everything you hear but you should also not dismiss everything you hear.

- Anon

1411. God hangs the greatest weights upon the smallest wires.

- Francis Bacon

1412. He that will not apply new remedies must expect new evils; for time is the greatest innovator.

- Francis Bacon

1413. If people have split views about your work, I think it's flattering. I'd rather have them feel something about it than dismiss it.

- Stephen Sondheim

1414. The value of a man should be seen in what he gives and not in what he is able to receive.

- Albert Einstein

1415. Have a horse of your own and then you may borrow another's.

- Welsh Proverb

1416. Glutton: one who digs his grave with his teeth.

- French Proverb

1417. I know not with what weapons World War III will be fought, but World War IV will be fought with sticks and stones.

- Albert Einstein

1418. Concealing an illness is like keeping a beach ball under water.

- Karen Duffy

1419. God gives the nuts, but he doesn't crack them.

- German Proverb

1420. The secret of learning to be sick is this: Illness doesn't make you less of what you were. You are still you.

- Tony Snow

1421. A jug fills drop by drop.

- Buddha

1422. Life's Tragedy is that we get old too soon and wise too late.

- Benjamin Franklin

1423. Acclaim is a distraction.

- James Broughton

1424. Half a loaf is better than a full loaf tomorrow.

- John Heywood

1425. Art is the fatal net which catches these strange moments on the wing like mysterious butterflies, fleeing the innocence and distraction of common men.

- Giorgio de Chirico

1426. Go to the door that's open, not the one that's closed.

- Anon

1427. A casual stroll through the lunatic asylums shows that faith does not prove anything.

- Friedrich William Nietzsche

1428. It is forbidden to kill: therefore all murders are punished unless they kill in large numbers and to the sound of trumpets.

- Voltaire

1429. He is not wise that is not wise for himself.

- English Proverb

1430. Not enough is better than nothing.

- Anon

1431. He that lives on hope will die fasting.

- North American Proverb

1432. Don't see the truth, be the truth.

- Franz Kafka

1433. Don't cheat anyone, not even the world.

- Franz Kafka

1434. Every man carries two bags about with him, one in front and one behind, and both are packed full of faults. The bag in front contains his neighbors faults, the one behind his own. Hence it is that men do not see their own faults, but never fail to see those of others.

- Aesop

1435. Idleness is the beginning of all vice, the crown of all virtues.

- Franz Kafka

1436. He makes his home where living is best.

- Latin Proverb

1437. He that can't endure the bad will not live to see the good.

- Jewish Proverb

1438. Always be yourself, express yourself, have faith in yourself, do not go out and look for a successful personality and duplicate it.

- Bruce Lee

1439. The cosmos is a gigantic flywheel, making 10,000 revolutions a minute. Man is a sick fly taking a dizzy ride on it. Religion is the theory that the wheel was designed and set spinning to give him the ride.

– H. L. Mencken

1440. Fortune befriends the bold.

- Emily Dickinson

1441. Gossip is called gossip because it's not always the truth.

- Justin Timberlake

1442. He that is of the opinion money will do everything may well be suspected of doing everything for money.

- Benjamin Franklin

1443. Serenity isn't boredom. Drama addiction is.

- Anon

1444. When you hear hooves, don't expect a zebra.

- Anon

1445. There is a place where dreams survive.

- Stan Bush

1446. Our last thoughts before we sleep follow us into our slumber. Make the most of your last thoughts.

- Lisa Nichols

1447. Always do sober what you said you would do drunk. That will teach ya.

- Ernest Hemingway

1448. We drink to drown our sorrows, but sorrows swim.

- Anon

1449. Drinking your problems away is like using an anesthetic on a wound. It numbs the pain, but you still need to treat the problem.

- Anon

1450. We cannot be blameless in our drunken actions, because we chose to put the first drink in our bodies.

- Anon

1451. What is said while drunk has been thought beforehand.

- Anon

1452. You choose to drink, so you can choose to stop.

- Anon

1453. Nobody wakes up and is suddenly an alcoholic.

- Anon

1454. As long as habit and routine dictate the pattern of living, new dimensions of the soul will not emerge.

- Henry Van Dyke

1455. You can search throughout the entire universe for someone who is more deserving of your love and affection that you are yourself, and that person is not to be found anywhere. You yourself, as much as anybody in the entire universe deserve your love and affection.

- Buddha

1456. Never trust a brilliant idea until it survives the hangover.

- Ernest Hemingway

1457. When you're finished changing, you're finished.

- Benjamin Franklin

1458. A great pretend is a fragile construct.

- Anon

1459. What's a sundial in the shade?

- Benjamin Franklin

1460. Without the element of uncertainty, the bringing off of even the greatest triumph would be dull, routine and eminently unsatisfying.

- J. Paul Getty

1461. If you spend too much time think about a thing, you will never get it done.

- Bruce Lee

1462. Time is money.

- Benjamin Franklin

1463. The finest warrior hardly needs to know how to construct a rifle or understand the chemistry of gunpowder

- Anon

1464. If you are happy, you don't need drugs. If you're not, then they aren't going to help.

- Anon

1465. Drugs are a bet with your mind.

- Jim Morrison

1466. Read not to contradict and confute, nor to believe and take for granted… but to weigh and consider.

- Francis Bacon

1467. It takes as much energy to wish as it does to plan.

- Eleanor Roosevelt

1468. All stories, if continued far enough, end in death, and he is no true-story teller who would keep that from you.

- Ernest Hemingway

1469. The man who is always talking about being a gentleman never is one.

- R.S. Surtees

1470. Friendship increases in not visiting friends, but in visiting them seldom.

- Francis Bacon

1471. A penny saved is a penny earned.

- Benjamin Franklin

1472. Write your injuries in dust, your benefits in marble.

- Benjamin Franklin

1473. To live is so startling, it leaves time for little else.

- Emily Dickinson

1474. No one is cockier than one who's bad at what he does.

- Anon

1475. Talking about oneself is a means of concealing one's insecurities.

- Anon

1476. We only brag about what we know won't last.

- Anon

1477. Opportunity makes a thief.

- Francis Bacon

1478. A fool always finds a greater fool who admires him, and flatterers live at the expense of the listeners.

- Anon

1479. As soon as you say you got what you wanted, you lose it— success, ambition, drive. The claiming of it makes it disappear.

- Anon

1480. I fear not the man who has practiced 10,000 kicks once, but I fear the man who has practiced one kick 10,000 times.

- Bruce Lee

1481. When dealing with people, remember you are not dealing with creatures of logic but creatures of emotion.

- Dale Carnegie

1482. Goals must never be from your ego, but problems that cry for a solution.

- Robert H. Schuller

1483. I'm not in this world to live up to your expectations and you're not in this world to live up to mine.

- Bruce Lee

1484. Emotion can be a straightjacket.

- Anon

1485. Emotion, like all fragile things, must be handled with care.

- Anon

1486. A disembodied emotion is a non-existent one.

- Theodule Ribot

1487. He that maketh haste to be rich shall not be innocent.

- Bible – Proverbs 28:20

1488. When you start to develop your powers of empathy and imagination, the whole world opens up to you.

- Susan Sarandon

1489. He that plants thorns must never expect to gather roses.

- English Proverb

1490. Suffering is only intolerable when nobody cares.

- Cicely Saunders

1491. Offers sound so appealing if they involve running away.

- Anon

1492. The eternal mystery of the world is its comprehensibility...the fact that it is comprehensible is a miracle.

- Albert Einstein

1493. Don't go somewhere that's got no answers.

- Anon

1494. Punctuated Equilibrium – We are not guaranteed Earth. We must earn this world.

- Stephen Jay Gould

1495. Justice cannot be for one side alone, but must be for both.
- Eleanor Roosevelt

1496. Neither by nature, then, nor contrary to nature do the virtues arise in us; nature gives us the capacity to receive them, and this capacity is brought to maturity by habit.
- Aristotle

1497. When we try to escape from our mistakes, we actually tend to run toward them.
- Anon

1498. If we don't empower ourselves with knowledge, then we're gonna be led down a garden path.
- Fran Drescher

1499. The same sun and moon shine on us no matter where we are in the world.
- Anon

1500. He that seeks trouble never misses.
- English Proverb

1501. As soon as men decide that all means are permitted to fight an evil, then their good becomes indistinguishable from the evil that they set out to destroy.
- Christopher Dawson

1502. To enter into your own mind, you need to be armed to the teeth.
- Paul Valery

1503. A belief in a supernatural source of evil is not necessary; mankind alone is quite capable of every wickedness imaginable.
- Anon

1504. There is scarcely a single man sufficiently aware to know all the evil he does.
- Duc de la Rochefoucauld

1505. It is .0000001 percent of the people who make 99.9999 percent of the important decisions of the world.
- Alan Moore

1506. When life is too easy for us, we must beware or we may not be ready to meet the blows which sooner or later come to everyone, rich or poor.

- Eleanor Roosevelt

1507. There are no necessary evils, only weak compromises.

- Anon

1508. Man is neither good or bad; he is born with instinct and abilities.

– Honore de Balzac

1509. It is better to travel well than to arrive.

- Buddha

1510. If all pulled in one direction, the world would keel over.

- Yiddish Proverb

1511. He who asks is a fool for five minutes, but he who does not ask remains a fool forever.

- Chinese Proverb

1512. If the patient dies, the doctor has killed him, but if he gets well, the saints have saved him.

- Italian Proverb

1513. An exaggeration is a truth that has lost its temper.

- Kahil Gibran

1514. He who cannot agree with his enemies is controlled by them.

- Chinese Proverb

1515. We can exaggerate our failures to justify them.

- Anon

1516. Exaggeration is a blood relation to falsehood and nearly as blameable.

- Hosea Ballou

1517. Nothing is absolute, with the debatable exceptions of this statement and death.

- John Ralston Saul

1518. Several excuses are always less convincing than one.

- Aldous Huxley

1519. Empty souls tend to extreme opinions.

- William Butler Yeats

1520. If you are good at making excuses, you are rarely good at anything else.

- Anon

1521. If two men ride a horse, one must ride behind.

- Anon

1522. If you believe the doctors, nothing is wholesome; if you believe the theologians, nothing is innocent; if you believe the soldiers, nothing is safe.

- Lord Salisbury

1523. Extremes, though contrary, have the like effects. Extreme heat kills, and so extreme cold: extreme love breeds satiety, and so extreme hatred; and too violent rigor tempts chastity, as does too much license.

- George Chapman

1524. Logical consequences are the scarecrows of fools and the beacons of wise men.

- T.H. Huxley.

1525. Just because a million people believe in a dumb idea, that doesn't change the fact that it's a dumb idea.

- Anon

1526. The deepest sin against the human mind is to believe things without evidence.

- T.H. Huxley

1527. It takes many good deeds to build a reputation and only one to lose it.

- Benjamin Franklin

1528. Happy families are all alike; every unhappy family is unhappy in its own way.

- Leo Tolstoy

1529. Good fame is like fire; when you have kindled you may easily preserve it; but if you extinguish it, you will not easily kindle it again.

- Francis Bacon

1530. Those who cheer today may hurl stones tomorrow.

- Anon

1531. If you are planning for a year, sow rice; if you are planning for a decade, plant trees; if you are planning for a lifetime, educate people.

- Chinese Proverb

1532. It's easier to resist at the beginning than at the end.

- Leonardo da Vinci

1533. Once the toothpaste is out of the tube, it's awfully hard to get it back in.

- Anon

1534. It is easier to forgive an enemy than to forgive a friend.

- William Blake
(Jerusalem)

1535. Unforgiveness prolongs past mistakes.

- Anon

1536. It is well, when judging a friend, to remember that he is judging you with the same godlike and superior impartiality.

- Arnold Bennett

1537. In a calm sea, every man is a pilot.

- Spanish Proverb

1538. If you believe everything you read, better not read.

- Japanese Proverb

1539. In baiting a mousetrap with cheese, always leave room for the mouse.

- Greek Proverb

1540. To appreciate heaven, it's good for a person to have some 15 minutes of hell.

- Will Carleton

1541. It is a bold mouse that nestles in the cat's ear.

- English Proverb

1542. God must love the common man, he made so many of them.

- Abraham Lincoln

1543. God does not play dice.

- Albert Einstein

1544. A goal is not always meant to be reached, it often serves simply as something to aim at.

- Bruce Lee

1545. The heart will break, but broken live on.

- Lord Byron

1546. 'Did you gut the pillow with a knife?' What were the results?'
'Feathers,' she said. Feathers; everywhere, Father.' '
Now I want you to go back and gather up every last feather,'
'Well,' she said, 'it can't be done. The wind took them all over.'
'And that,' said Father O' Rourke, 'is gossip!'

- Father Brendan Flynn
(Doubt)

1547. Gossip: humanity's most pointless sin. It tends to be the origin of all others.

- Anon

1548. Most rumors start by remembering the past wrong.

- Anon

1549. People always whip themselves into a gossiping frenzy of misinformed speculation.

- Anon

1550. Bullying in school used to be name-calling or physical abuse. Now people just spread spiteful rumors.

- Anon

1551. In matters of truth and justice, there is no difference between large and small problems, for issues concerning the treatment of people are all the same.

- Albert Einstein

1552. There's more power in rumors than in truth. A fact can be disproven, but a rumor lingers forever.

- Anon

1553. Remember, the only thing that gets thicker when spread is rumor.

- Anon

1554. Nothing is so firmly believed as that which we least know.

- Montaigne

1555. Grief for the dead is mad; it is an injury to the living, and the dead know it not.

- Xenophon

1556. A death isn't like losing a job or getting a divorce. There is no "getting over it." You have to integrate it into your life and live with it. It isn't like stopping a bomb going off. It is the bomb going off, and you have to survive somehow.

- Anon

1557. How many legs does a dog have if you call the tail a leg? Four. Calling a tail a leg doesn't make it a leg.

- Abraham Lincoln

1558. Slow but steady wins the race.

- Aesop

1559. Outside show is a poor substitute for inner worth.

- Aesop

1560. A wise man can learn more from a foolish question than a fool can learn from a wise answer.

- Bruce Lee

1561. Health is the greatest gift, contentment the greatest wealth, faithfulness the best relationship.

- Buddha

1562. He who joyfully marches to music in rank and file has already earned my contempt. He has been given a large brain by mistake, since for him the spinal cord would suffice.

- Albert Einstein

1563. Given a choice between grief and nothing, I'd choose grief.

- William Faulkner

1564. Men are nearly always willing to believe what they wish.

- Julius Caesar

1565. It is a long road that has no turning.

- Irish Proverb

1566. To his dog, every man is Napoleon; hence the constant popularity of dogs.

- Aldous Huxley

1567. Laughter is the cheapest medicine.

- Lord Byron

1568. Notice that the stiffest tree is most easily cracked, while the bamboo or willow survives by bending with the wind.

- Bruce Lee

1569. Many forms of Government have been tried and will be in this world of sin and woe. No one pretends that democracy is perfect or all-wise. Indeed, it has been said that democracy is the worst form of government except all those other forms that have been tried from time to time.

- Winston Churchill

1570. All gods are homemade, and it is we who pull their strings, and so, give them the power to pull ours.

- Aldous Huxley

1571. It is easier to prevent bad habits than to break them.

- Benjamin Franklin

1572. Those that can make you believe in absurdities can make you commit atrocities.

- Voltaire

1573. Gradually changing habits makes more difference than changing them all at once.

- Ian K. Smith

1574. Success is to be measured not so much by the position that one has reached in life as by the obstacles which he has overcome.

- Booker T. Washington

1575. Our suggestibility knows no limits.

- David Mamet

1576. It's not that I'm so smart, it's just that I stay with problems longer.

- Albert Einstein

1577. I never see what has been done; I only see what remains to be done.

- Buddha

1578. I am indebted to my father for living, but to my teacher for living well.

- Alexander the Great

1579. Nothing ever comes to one, that is worth having, except as a result of hard work.

- Booker T. Washington

1580. Remember not only to say the right thing in the right place, but far more difficult still, to leave unsaid the wrong thing at the tempting moment.

- Benjamin Franklin

1581. The best way to get a bad law repealed is to enforce it strictly.

- Abraham Lincoln

1582. It is thrifty to prepare today for the wants of tomorrow.

- Aesop

1583. We all like to hide behind hard work, but hard work doesn't guarantee results.

- Steve Woodward

1584. Love, friendship, respect do not unite people as much as common hatred for something.

> \- Anton Chekhov

1585. Men often applaud an imitation and hiss the real thing.

> \- Aesop

1586. No one is born hating. People must learn to hate.

> \- Nelson Mandela

1587. Is the pious loved by the gods because it is pious, or is it pious because they love it?

> \- Plato

1588. Virtue is persecuted more by the wicked than it is loved by the good.

> \- Buddha

1589. No morality can be founded on authority, even if the authority were divine.

> \- A.J. Ayer

1590. Heaven cannot brook two suns, nor earth two masters.

> \- Alexander the Great

1591. Success in life is founded upon attention to the small things rather than to the large things; to the everyday things nearest to us rather than to the things that are remote and uncommon.

> \- Booker T. Washington

1592. Psychoanalysis is a technique to cure excessively suffering individuals of the unconsciously misdirected desires that weave around their private webs of unreal terror and ambivalent attractions.

> \- Joseph Campbell

1593. It is not enough to run, one must start in time.

> \- French Proverb

1594. It is not the horse that draws the cart, but the oats.

> \- Russian Proverb

1595. I shall allow no man to belittle my soul by making me hate him.

> \- Booker T. Washington

1596. Know your limitations. Never accept them.

- Anon

1597. There are two ways of exerting one's strength; one is pushing down, the other is pulling up.

- Booker T. Washington

1598. Not all who hesitate are lost. The psyche has many secrets in reserve. And these are not disclosed unless required.

- Joseph Campbell

1599. It is an equal failing to trust everybody and to trust nobody.

- English Proverb

1600. It is hard to pay for bread that has been eaten.

- Danish Proverb

1601. It's so easy to manipulate, but it's nearly always clear that you are being manipulated.

- John Boorman

1602. It is better to be born a beggar than a fool.

- Spanish Proverb

1603. Hypocrisy is the outside of cynicism.

- Mason Cooley

1604. It is better to conceal one's knowledge than to reveal one's ignorance.

- Spanish Proverb

1605. Fate is the word cowards use to describe the things we are too weak to change.

- Friedrich Nietzsche

1606. It is sweet to drink but bitter to pay for.

- Irish Proverb

1607. Life is a foreign language all men mispronounce.

- Christopher Morley

1608. Keep a thing for seven years and you'll find a use for it.

- Irish Proverb

1609. When elephants fight, it is the ground that suffers.

- Anon

1610. Every man who knows how to read has it in his power to magnify himself, to multiply the ways in which he exists, to make his life full, significant and interesting.

- Aldous Huxley

1611. No greater injury can be done to any youth than to let him feel that because he belongs to this or that race, he will be advanced in life regardless of his own merits or efforts.

- Booker T. Washington

1612. Be thou the rainbow in the storms of life.

- Lord Byron

1613. Man goes into the noisy crowd to drown his own clamor of silence.

- Radindranath Tagore

1614. The difference between stupidity and genius is that genius has its limits.

- Albert Einstein

1615. If you hate a person, you hate something in him that is part of yourself. What isn't part of ourselves doesn't disturb us.

- Hermann Hesse

1616. Like a lame man's legs that hang limp is a proverb in the mouth of a fool.

- Bible – Proverbs 26:7

1617. Kill not the goose that lays the golden egg.

- English Proverb

1618. The quarrel of friends are the opportunities of foes.

- Anon

1619. Life is a bridge. Cross over it, but build no house on it.

- Indian Proverb

1620. Life without a friend is death without a witness.

- Spanish Proverb

1621. He who wishes to fight must first count the cost.

- Sun Tzu

1622. If the actual victory is long and far, you will exhaust your strength if you face it head on.

- Sun Tzu

1623. Hell isn't merely paved with good intentions; it's walled and roofed with them. Yes, and furnished too.

- Aldous Huxley

1624. Cleverness has never been associated with long delays.

- Anon

1625. If you do what you always do, you get what you always get.

- Anon

1626. The magic of first love is our ignorance that it can't ever end.

- Benjamin Disraeli

1627. Hunger is the best cook.

- Italian Proverb

1628. I don't believe in depriving myself of any food or being imprisoned by a diet.

- Joely Fisher

1629. The trouble with always trying to preserve the health of the body is that it is so difficult to do without destroying the health of the mind.

- Gilbert K. Chesterton

1630. To a hungry man, there is no bad bread.

- French Proverb

1631. Oat bread today is better than cake tomorrow.

- Yugoslavian Proverb

1632. The radical of one century is the conservative of the next.

- Anon

1633. Listen to the sound of a river and you will get a trout.

- Irish Proverb

1634. Many would die before they think. And they do.

- Bertrand Russell

1635. Live with wolves, and you learn to howl.

- Spanish Proverb

1636. Mankind is divisible into two great classes; hosts and guests.

- Max Beerbohm

1637. Never cut what can be united.

- Portuguese Proverb

1638. The will to be or become has been replaced by the will to seem.

- Alfred Adler

1639. Men count up the faults of those who keep them waiting.

- French Proverb

1640. False face must hide what the false heart doth know.

- William Shakespeare

1641. Mere words do not feed the friars.

- Irish Proverb

1642. A strong sense of identity gives man an idea he can do no wrong; too little accomplishes the same.

- Djuna Barnes

1643. How frightful is man's condition! There is not one of his joys which does not come from some ignorance or other.

- Honor de Balzac

1644. Point me out the happy man and I will point you out either egotism, selfishness evil – or else absolute ignorance.

- Graham Greene

1645. We are all ill-equipped to comprehend the very small and very large.

- Richard Dawkins

1646. More grows in the garden than the gardener knows he has sown.

- Spanish Proverb

1647. Whenever two people meet, there are really six people, there is each man as he sees himself, each man as the other sees him, and each man as he really is.

- William James

1648. No man limps because another is hurt.

- Danish Proverb

1649. Propaganda does not deceive people' it merely helps them to deceive themselves.

- Eric Hoffer

1650. No rose is without a thorn or a love without a rival.

- Turkish Proverb

1651. One father is more than a hundred schoolmasters.

- English Proverb

1652. Much reading is an oppression of the mind, and extinguishes the natural candle, which is the reason of so many senseless scholars in the world.

- William Penn
(Fruits of a Father's Love)

1653. To live in fear is to not live at all.

- Anon

1654. One should look long and carefully at oneself before one considers judging others.

- Moliere

1655. We may often be of more consequence in our own eyes than in the eyes of others.

- Anon

1656. Man differs from other animals in that he is the most imitative of creatures, and he learns his earliest lessons by imitation. Inborn in all of us is this instinct.

- Aristotle

1657. Winning is a habit. So is losing.

- Vince Lombardi

1658. Giving a phenomenon a label does not explain it.

- Taylor Caldwell

1659. Mimicry is the most common form of flattery but it is not your own.

- Anon

1660. If you love life, don't waste time, for time is what life made up of.

- Bruce Lee

1661. The scientific approach to the phenomenon of human nature enables us to be ignorant without being frightened and without therefore having to invent all sorts of weird theories to explain away all the gaps in knowledge.

- D. W. Winnicott

1662. It's more fun to arrive to a conclusion than to justify it.

- Malcolm Forbes

1663. Blame is just a lazy way for a person to make sense of chaos.

- Doug Coupland

1664. Immortal mortals and mortal immortals, living the others death and dying the other's life.

- Herodotus.

1665. Death cancels everything but truth, and strips a man of everything but genius and virtue. It is a sort of natural canonization.

- William Hazlitt

1666. There are only two mistakes one can make along the road to truth; not going all the way and not starting.

- Buddha

1667. No one means all he says, and yet very few say all they mean, for words are slippery and thought is viscous.

- Henry Brooks Adams

1668. One flower will not make a garland.

- French Proverb

1669. It is commonly said that the most powerful weapon is the truth, but I think it can be the twisting of truths.

- Anon

1670. A lie is the only substitute for the truth. It's not a great one, but it's the only one known and seems to be used just as often.

- Anon

1671. Three things cannot be long hidden: the sun, the moon, and the truth.

- Buddha

1672. All that is buried is not dead.

- Olive Schreiner

1673. No mistake is more common and more fatuous than appealing to logic in cases which are beyond her jurisdiction.

- Samuel Butler

1674. The universe is not only queerer than we suppose but queerer than we can suppose.

- J.B.S. Halone.

1675. Love is like heaven but can hurt like hell.

- Anon

1676. The heart has its reason that reason cannot answer.

- Anon

1677. Your perfect love is rarely convenient love.

- Anon

1678. What the mass media offers is not popular art, but entertainment which is intended to be consumed like food, forgotten, and replaced by a new dish.

- W. H. Auden

1679. For we do not easily expect evil of those whom we love most.

- Peter Abelard

1680. Media exist to invest our lives with artificial perceptions and arbitrary values.

- Marshall McLuhan

1681. The mask if worn long enough will be the face.

- Stephen Fry

1682. One generation plants the trees; another gets the shade.

- Chinese Proverb

1683. Behind every face, the mental emptiness deepen.

- T.S. Elliott

1684. One joy scatters a thousand griefs.

- Chinese Proverb

1685. Home is the place, where when you have to go there, they have to take you in.

- Robert Frost

1686. Example is not the main thing in influencing others, it is the only thing.

- Albert Schweitzer

1687. I mean there is something sort of insincere about changing your nose. If that's all that makes or breaks you, the shape of a piece of cartilage? I mean if you're going to go through life building everything on that.

- Felice
(After The Fall)

1688. If it has to choose who is to be crucified, the crowd will always save Barabbas.

- Jean Cocteau
(Le Rappel a l'ordre)

1689. One should go invited to a friend in good fortune, and uninvited in misfortune.

- Swedish Proverb

1690. Life is like the children's game of Snakes and Ladders—except there are a lot more snakes and they drop you farther down.

- Anon

1691. A lack of money is the root of all evil.

- Mark Twain

1692. Thousands of candles can be lighted from a single candle, and the life of the candle will not be shortened.

- Buddha

1693. At least I have the modesty to admit that lack of modesty is one of my failings.

- Hector Berlioz

1694. Comedy is tragedy that happens to other people.

- Angela Carter

1695. Nothing helps a bad mood like spreading it around.

- Bill Watterson

1696. The New Age? Ha! It's just the old age stuck in a microwave oven for fifteen seconds.

- James Randi

1697. Only the wearer knows where the shoe pinches.

- English Proverb

1698. Ridicule is the only weapon to unintelligent propositions.

- Richard Dawkins

1699. There are only two classes of pedestrians in these days of reckless motor traffic – the quick and the dead.

- James Dewar

1700. The hottest place in Hell is reserved for those who remain neutral in times of great moral conflict.

- Martin Luther King Jr

1701. Innocence always calls mutely for protection, when we would be so much wiser to guard ourselves against it.

- Graham Greene

1702. If you are neutral in situations of injustice, you have chosen the side of the oppressor. If an elephant has its foot on the tail of a mouse and you say that you are neutral, the mouse will not appreciate the neutrality.

- Desmond Tutu

1703. We live in a universe in which there are laws, just as there is a law of gravity. If you fall off a building it doesn't matter if you're a good person or a bad person, you're going to hit the ground.

- Michael Bernard Beckwith

1704. Put silk on a goat, and it's still a goat.

- Irish Proverb

1705. Innocence is like a leper who has lost his bell, wandering the world meaning no harm.

- Graham Greene

1706. The past is foreign country. They do things differently there.

- L. Hartley

1707. Dreams are always set in the past.

- A. Phillips

1708. Memory is deceptive. It is colored by today's events.

- Albert Einstein

1709. Youth is vivid rather than happy, but memory always remember the happy things.

- Bernard Lovell

1710. What is the appropriate behavior for a man or a woman in the midst of this world, where each person is clinging to his piece of debris? What's the proper salutation between people as they each other in the flood?

- Buddha

1711. The present is an age of talkers, and not of doers, and the reason is, that the world is growing old. We are so far advanced in the Arts and Sciences, that we live in retrospect, and dote on past achievement.

- William Hazlitt

1712. Nostalgia is a self-defense mechanism to cast our minds back to a more relaxing time that probably never existed.

- Anon

1713. He who rides a tiger is afraid to dismount.

- Chinese Proverb

1714. If one were to order all mankind to choose the best set rules in the world, each group would, after due consideration, regard its own as being by far the best.

- George Herbert

1715. Fear is the thought of admitted inferiority.

-Elbert Hubbard

1716. Rain beats a leopard's skin, but it does not wash off the spots.

- Ashanti Proverb

1717. A wrong concept misleads the understanding; a wrong deed degrades the whole man, and may eventually demolish the structure of the human ego.

- Muhammed Iqbal

1718. Fear is pain arising from the anticipation of evil.

- Aristotle

1719. You know you've got paranoia when you can't think of anything that's your fault.

- Robert M. Hutchins

1720. Your pain is the breaking of the shell that encloses your understanding.

- Khalil Gibran

1721. To him is in fear, everything rustles.

- Sophocles

1722. If we scare ourselves with the nonexistent, we stand no chance facing real danger.

- Anon

1723. Holding onto anger is like grasping a hot coal with the intent of throwing it at someone else; you are the one who gets burned.

- Buddha

1724. We tend to perfume and reinterpret; meanwhile imagining that all the flies in the ointment, all the hairs in the soup, are the faults of some unpleasant someone else.

- Joseph Campbell

1725. The mind will always rebel at a direct command – go to sleep, fall in love, stop crying, don't get angry, say you're sorry, take back what you said, you don't have the guts to do that, listen, stop talking, relax, be quiet, wake up.

- David Mamet

1726. Through pride, we are even deceiving ourselves.

- Carl Jung

1727. The first half of our lives is ruined by our parents; the second half by our children.

- Anon

1728. You will not be punished for your anger, you will be punished by your anger.

- Buddha

1729. A perfection of means, and confusion of aims, seems to be our main problem.

- Albert Einstein

1730. A pedestal is as much a prison as any small, confined space.

- Gloria Steinem

1731. I would do anything to be muscular except exercise or eat right.

– Steve Martin

1732. Those who think they have no time for bodily exercise will sooner or later have to find time for illness.

- Edward Stanley

1733. Nearly all men can stand adversity, but if you want to test a man's character, give him power.

- Abraham Lincoln

1734. Rats desert a sinking ship.

- French Proverb

1735. What is the matter with the poor is Poverty; what is the matter with the rich is Uselessness.

- George Bernard Shaw

1736. I'm not afraid of the darkness outside but the darkness inside.
- Shelagh Delaney

1737. It's not what's said that decides a relationship but what's unsaid.
- Anon

1738. The gods can only laugh when one prays for money.
- Japanese Proverb

1739. Love will find a way through paths where wolves fear to prey.
- Lord Byron

1740. When Hitler attacked the Jews I was not a Jew, therefore I was not concerned. And when Hitler attacked Catholics, I was not a Catholic, and therefore, I was not concerned. And when Hitler attacked the unions and the industrialists, I was not a member of the unions and I was not concerned. Then, Hitler attacked me and the Protestant church – and there was nobody left to be concerned.
- Martin Niemoller

1741. Intolerance of groups is often, strangely enough, exhibited more strongly against small differences than against fundamental ones.
- Sigmund Freud

1742. Work is only noticed when it's not done.
- Anon

1743. We know what happens to people who stay in the middle of the road. They get run down.
- Aneurin Bevan

1744. If people are good only because they fear punishment, and hope for reward, then we are a sorry lot indeed.
- Albert Einstein

1745. It is human nature to instinctively rebel at obscurity or ordinariness.
- Taylor Caldwell

1746. Give a man a fish and you will feed him for a day. Give him religion and he will starve to death praying for a fish.
- George Carlin

1747. There's an invisible man living in the sky who watches everything you do. And the invisible man has a special list of ten things he does not want you to do. And if you do any of these ten things, he has a special place, full of fire and smoke and burning and torture and anguish, where he will send you to live and suffer and burn and choke and scream and cry forever and ever 'til the end of time!..... But he loves you!

- George Carlin

1748. He is poor indeed that can promise nothing.

- Thomas Fuller

1749. Daughter am I in my mother's house but mistress in my own.

- Rupert Kipling

1750. Since we cannot get what we like, let us like what we can get.

- Spanish Proverb

1751. Habit and routine have an unbelievable power to waste and destroy.

- Henri de Lubac

1752. Small children give you headache, big children heartache.

- Russian Proverb

1753. I hate having my life disrupted by routine.

- Caskie Stinnett

1754. In every aspect of life, there is a security blanket, a thumb to suck, a skirt to hold.

- Isaac Asimov

1755. Just because something is comfortable doesn't mean it is right, safe, healthy, or real.

- Anon

1756. We need pessimists as much as we need optimists. An optimist invented the airplane. A pessimist invented the parachute.

- Anon

1757. There is pleasure in the pathless woods, there is rapture in the lonely shore, there is society where none intrudes, by the deep sea and music in its roar, I love not Man the less, but Nature more.

- Lord Byron

1758. We cannot change anything until we accept it.

- Carl Jung

1759. Nothing fortifies skepticism more than the fact that there are some who are not skeptics; if all were so, they would be wrong.

- Blaise Pascal

1760. A fool is a man who never tried an experiment in his life.

- Erasmus Darwin

1761. A new scientific truth does not triumph by convincing its opponents and making them see the light, but rather because its opponents eventually die, and a new generation grows up that is familiar with it.

- Max Planck

1762. Science is organized knowledge.

- Anon

1763. Science is built up of facts, as a house is built of stones; but an accumulation of facts is no more a science than a heap of stones is a house.

- Henri Poincare

1764. Science is not to open the door to infinite wisdom, but to set a limit to infinite error.

- Bertolt Brecht

1765. Probable impossibilities are to be preferred to improbable possibilities.

- Aristotle

1766. Truth exists; only lies are invented.

- Anon

1767. They say the hardest part of a relationship is ending it but it isn't. That's the easiest part. All you have to do is stop trying. That's why nearly all of them end. The hardest part is keeping it.

- Aaron Chenowith

1768. A desperate disease requires a dangerous remedy.

- Guy Fawkes

1769. Fortunately, analysis is not the only way to resolve inner conflicts. Life itself still remains a very effective therapist.

- Karen Horney

1770. Everyone suffers wrongs for which there is no remedy.

- Edgar Watson Howe

1771. It is impossible for a man to organize his life with repressions.

- Arthur Miller

1772. Some people are masters of money, and some its slaves.

- Russian Proverb

1773. Hateful to me as the gates of Hades is the man who hides one thing in his heart and says another.

– Homer

1774. Sometimes I go about pitying myself, and all the time I am being carried on great wings across the sky.

- Ojibway Saying

1775. Your character is what you are, your reputation is what others think you are.

- John Wooden

1776. It is a revenge the devil sometimes takes upon the virtuous, that he entraps them by the force of the very passion they have suppressed and think themselves superior to.

- George Santayana

1777. Speak not of my debts unless you mean to pay them.

- English Proverb

1778. The road to a friend's house is never long.

- Danish Proverb

1779. The tallest blade of grass is the first to be cut by the scythe.

- Russian Proverb

1780. Never in the field of human conflict was so much owed by so many to so few. A medal glitters, but it also casts a shadow.

- Winston Churchill

1781. Sweet is wine but sour is the payment.

- Irish Proverb

1782. He that studieth revenge keepeth his own wounds green, which otherwise would heal and do well.

- John Milton

1783. Somewhere, something incredible is waiting to be known.

- Carl Sagan

1784. The gem cannot be polished without friction, nor man perfected without trials.

- Chinese Proverb

1785. A man's true secrets are more secret to himself than to others.

- Paul Valery

1786. An eye for an eye leaves everyone blind.

- Anon

1787. The girl who can't dance says the band can't play.

- Yiddish Proverb

1788. Three can keep a secret, if two of them are dead.

- Benjamin Franklin

1789. Some do not choose, they settle. They go where they are pushed or pulled.

- Anon

1790. If you look at life like rolling a dice, then my situation now, as it stands – yeah, it may only be a 3. If I jack that in now, go for something bigger and better, yeah, I could easily roll a 6 – no problem, I could roll a 6... I could also roll a 1.

– Tim
(The Office)

1791. The tongue is to be feared more than the sword.

– Japanese Proverb

1792. The tongue kills without drawing blood.

- Chinese Proverb

1793. Facts do not cease to exist because they are ignored.
                                        - Aldous Huxley

1794. The wise adapt themselves to circumstances, as water molds
      itself to the pitcher.
                                        - Chinese Proverb

1795. The wise man sits on the hole in his carpet.
                                        - Persian Proverb

1796. Because I am a woman, I must make unusual efforts to succeed.
      If I fail, no one will say, "She doesn't have what it takes."
      They will say, "Women don't have what it takes.
                                        - Clare Boothe Luce

1797. The turtle lays thousands of eggs without anyone knowing, but
      when the hen lays an egg, the whole country is informed.
                                        - Malay Proverb

1798. The well fed does not understand the lean.
                                        - Irish Proverb

1799. So long as men worship the Caesars and Napoleons, Caesars and
      Napoleons will duly arise and make them miserable.
                                        - Aldous Huxley

1800. Few things can help an individual more than to place
      responsibility on him, and to let him know that you trust him.
                                        - Booker T. Washington

1801. I am dying with the help of too many physicians.
                                        - Alexander the Great

1802. Dignity does not consist in possessing honors, but in deserving
      them.
                                        - Aristotle
1803. Important principles may, and must, be inflexible.
                                        - Abraham Lincoln

1804. The whisper of a pretty girl can be heard further than the roar of
      a lion.
                                        - Arabian Proverb

1805. Men often grudge others what they cannot enjoy themselves.

- Aesop

1806. Roll on, deep and dark blue ocean, roll. Ten thousand fleets sweep over thee in vain. Man marks the Earth with ruin, but his control stops with the shore.

- Lord Byron

1807. The Bible teaches us that woman brought sin and death into the world, which she precipitated the fall of the race...marriage for her was to be a condition of bondage, maternity a period of suffering and anguish, and in silence and subjection, she was to play the role of a dependent on man's bounty for all her material wants.

- Elizabeth Cady Stanton

1808. The wolf loses his teeth, but not his inclinations.

- Spanish Proverb

1809. If you can't sleep, then get up and do something instead of lying there worrying. It's the worry that gets you, not the lack of sleep.

- Dale Carnegie

1810. I am not afraid of the lions led by the sheep. I am afraid of the sheep lead by the lions.

- Alexander the Great

1811. Many a man is praised for his reserve and so-called shyness when he is simply to proud to risk making a fool of himself.

- J.B. Priestly

1812. Some protect the here and now. Others protect the long-term invisible, unlikely, or non-existent.

- Anon

1813. Skilled or unskilled, we all scribble poems.

- Horace

1814. Foolish people do not understand that what is seen is merely their own mind.

- Mahayana Buddhist texts

1815. I cannot and will not cut my conscience to fit this year's fashions.

– Lillian Hellman

1816. The world would not make a racehorse of a donkey.

- Irish Proverb

1817. A ruffled mind makes a restless pillow.

- Charlotte Bronte

1818. There are many paths to the top of the mountain, but the view is always the same.

- Chinese Proverb

1819. Course we're all gonna die some day. But do we have to pay for it? Do we have to actually throw hard-earned dollars down on the counter and say, "Please Mr. Merchant-of-Death, please, sell me something that'll stink up my breath and my clothes and fry my lungs.

- Chewies Gum Rep
(Clerks)

1820. If we reduce social life to the smallest possible unit we will find that there is no social life in the company of one.

- Jerzy Kosinski

1821. There is nothing to it. You only have to hit the right notes at the right time and the instrument plays itself.

– Johann Sebastian Bach

1822. Though a tree grow ever so high, the falling leaves return to the ground.

- Malay Proverb

1823. To deny all, is to confess all.

- Spanish Proverb

1824. To talk without thinking is to shoot without aiming.

- English Proverb

1825. Particles, chaos, inertia, entropy. The universe doesn't give a damn.

- Anon

1826. To teach is to learn.

- Japanese Proverb

1827. You want to believe that there's one relationship in life that's beyond betrayal. A relationship that's beyond that kind of hurt. And there isn't.

- Caleb Carr

1828. Eyes and ears are bad witnesses to men if they have souls that understand not their language.

- Anon

1829. The significance of man is that he is insignificant and is aware of it.

– Carl Becker

1830. Nostalgia often leads to idle speculation.

- Paul Getty

1831. Tomorrow is often the busiest day of the week.

- Spanish Proverb

1832. The only thing worse than not changing is regressing.

- Anon

1833. True nobility is in being superior to your previous self.

- Hindustani Proverb

1834. There's nothing worse than having everybody thinking alike, talking alike and having the same direction in mind. It gets stale that way.

- Alex Van Halen

1835. Trust in God but tie your camel.

- Muslim Proverb

1836. Sorrow is knowledge, those that know the most must mourn the deepest, the tree of knowledge is not the tree of life.

- Lord Byron

1837. Even a happy life cannot be without a measure of darkness and the word happy would lose its meaning if it were not balanced by sadness.

- Carl Jung

1838. Some stories are true that never happened.

- Elie Wiesel

1839. All stories, if continued far enough, end in death, and he is no true-story teller who would keep that from you.

- Ernest Hemingway

1840. Food can become such a point of anxiety - not because it's food, but just because you have anxiety. That's how eating disorders develop.

- Vanessa Carlton

1841. As the rich consume more and more, they are clearly not going to want to downgrade their own status.

- Susan George

1842. Refusal to believe until proof is given is a rational position; denial of all outside of our own limited experience is absurd.

- Annie Besant

1843. Those who will not reason are bigots, those who cannot are fools, those who dare not are slaves.

- Lord Byron

1844. Nothing can stress you out more than yourself.

- Anon

1845. The poor dog, in life the firmest friend. The first to welcome, foremost to defend.

- Lord Byron

1846. To be ambitious for wealth, and yet always expecting to be poor; to be always doubting your ability to get what you long for, is like trying to reach east by travelling west. There is no philosophy which will help man to succeed when he is always doubting his ability to do so, and thus attracting failure.

- Charles Baudouin

1847. If you have abandoned one faith, do not abandon all faith. There is always an alternative. Or is the same faith under another mask?

- Graham Greene

1848. If you criticize something then you have to have an alternative, but we do have to try and improve things.

- Linford Christie

1849. The most distressing thing that can happen to a prophet is to be proved wrong. The next most distressing thing is to be proved right.

- Aldous Huxley

1850. Ah, yes, superstition: it would appear to be cowardice in face of the supernatural.

- Anon

1851. Truth and oil always come to the surface.

– Spanish Proverb

1852. Our subconscious makes no dissimilarity between constructive and destructive thoughts. It takes what it is given.

- Tom Ryan

1853. Truth has a handsome countenance but torn garments.

- German Proverb

1854. Don't be superstitious. It will bring bad luck.

- Anon

1855. Truth is the safest lie.

- Jewish Proverb

1856. A bad book is as much of a labor to write as a good one, it comes as sincerely from the author's soul.

- Aldous Huxley

1857. I count him braver who overcomes his desires than him who conquers his enemies; for the hardest victory is over self.

- Aristotle

1858. The only way to keep your health is to eat what you don't want, drink what you don't like, and do what you'd rather not.

- Mark Twain

1859. Education is an ornament in prosperity and a refuge in adversity.

- Aristotle

1860. Two shorten the road.

- Irish Proverb

1861. Opportunities may knock only once but temptation leans on the doorbell.

- Anon

1862. Walk straight, my son – as the old crab said to the young crab.

- Irish Proverb

1863. What you cannot avoid, welcome.

- Chinese Proverb

1864. Superstition is rooted in the brain more deeply than skepticism.

- Johann Wolfgang von Goethe

1865. What breaks in a moment may take years to mend.

- Swedish Proverb

1866. It is a capital mistake to theorize before one has data. Insensibly one begins to twist facts to suit theories, instead of theories to suit facts.

- Sherlock Holmes
(A Scandal in Bohemia)

1867. What one knows is sometimes useful to forget.

- Latin Proverb

1868. Labor without joy is base. Labor without sorrow is base. Sorrow without labor is base.

- Anon

1869. When a father helps a son, both smile; but when a son must help his father, both cry.

- Jewish Proverb

1870. If there is anything that we wish to change in the child, we should first examine it and see whether it is not something that could better be changed in ourselves.

- Carl Jung

1871. If we could first know where we are, and whither we are tending, we could then better judge what to do, and how to do it.

- Abraham Lincoln

1872. When you have got an elephant by the hind legs and he is trying to run away, it's best to let him run.

- Abraham Lincoln

1873. In theory, there is no difference between theory and practice, but in practice, there is.

- Anon

1874. The healthy man does not torture others – generally it is the tortured who turn into others.

- Carl Jung

1875. When ill luck falls asleep, let none wake her.

- Italian Proverb

1876. No written law has ever been more binding than unwritten custom supported by popular opinion.

- Carrie Chapman Catt

1877. The pendulum of the mind alternates between sense and nonsense, not between right and wrong.

- Carl Jung

1878. When spider webs unite, they can tie up a lion.

- Ethiopian Proverb

1879. When the mouse laughs at the cat, there is a hole nearby.

- Nigerian Proverb

1880. When the apple is ripe, it will fall.

- Irish Proverb

1881. When the sword of rebellion is drawn, the sheath should be thrown away.

- English Proverb

1882. Nature abhors a vacuum.

- Francois Rabelais

1883. Tradition, long conditioned thinking, can bring about a fixation, a concept that one readily accepts, perhaps not with a great deal of thought.

- Jiddu Krishnamurti

1884. To make an apple pie from scratch, you must first invent the universe.

- Albert Einstein

1885. A common mistake that people make when trying to design something completely foolproof is to underestimate the ingenuity of complete fools.

- Douglas Adams

1886. Man is the only creature that consumes without producing.

- George Orwell

1887. Every man is said to have his peculiar ambition. Whether is be true or not, I can say for one that I have no other so great as that of being truly esteemed of my fellow men, by rendering myself worthy of their esteem.

- Abraham Lincoln

1888. The fact that we live at the bottom of a deep gravity well, on the surface of a gas covered planet going around a nuclear fireball ninety million miles away and think this is normal is some indication of how skewed our perspective tends to be.

- Douglas Adams

1889. Yesterday is but a dream, tomorrow is but a vision. But today well lived makes every yesterday a dream of happiness, and every tomorrow a vision of hope. Look well, therefore, to This Day.

- Sanskrit Proverb

1890. When you live next to the cemetery, you cannot weep for everyone.

- Russian Proverb

1891. Knowing your own darkness is the best method for dealing with the darknesses of other people.

- Carl Jung

1892. You cannot reason with a hungry belly, it has no ears.

- Greek Proverb

1893. Any excuse will serve a tyrant.

- Aesop

1894. Beware that you do not lose the substance by grasping at the shadow.

- Aesop

1895. The shoe that fits one person pinches another; there is no recipe for living that suits all cases.

- Carl Jung

1896. All men commend patience, although few are willing to practice it.

- Thomas Kempis

1897. Waiting is still an occupation. It's having nothing to wait for that is terrible.

- Cesare Pavese

1898. There is no greater pain than to remember a happy time when one is in misery.

- Dante Alighieri

1899. There is an eagle in me that wants to soar, and there is a hippopotamus in me that wants to wallow in the mud.

- Carl Sandburg

1900. We often give our enemies the means for our own destruction.

- Aesop

1901. When your enemy falls, don't rejoice- but don't pick him up either.

- Yiddish Proverb

1902. A lunatic cannot put out the sun by scribbling the word, 'darkness' on the walls of his cell.

- C. S. Lewis

1903. Where the tongue slips, it speaks the truth.

- Irish Proverb

1904. Who knows most, speaks least.

- Spanish Proverb

1905. Never trust the advice of a man in difficulties.

- Aesop

1906. When we start deceiving ourselves into thinking not that we want something or need something, not that it is a pragmatic necessity for us to have it, but that it is a moral imperative that we have it, then is when we join the fashionable madmen, and then is when the thin whine of hysteria is heard in the land, and then we are in trouble.

- Joan Didion

1907. Experience only teaches the teachable.

- Aldous Huxley

1908. It is a bit embarrassing to have been concerned with the human problem all one's life and find at the end that one has no more to offer by way of advice than "try to be a little kinder."

- Aldous Huxley

1909. Solitude is painful when one is young, but delightful when one is more mature.

- Albert Einstein

1910. A man who has not passed through the inferno of his passions has never overcome them.

- Carl Jung

1911. The Rum Tum Tugger is a Curious Cat:
If you set him on a mouse then he only wants a rat,
If you set him on a rat then he'd rather chase a mouse.

-T.S. Eliot
(Old Possum's Book of Practical Cats)

1912. It's easier to make war than to make peace.

- Georges Clemenceau

1913. War is all that is offered in a world in desperate need of healing.

- Anon

1914. You men may die, old men must.

- English Proverb

1915. The opposite of war isn't peace; it's creation.

- Anon

1916. What forgets is the axe, but the tree that has been axed will never forget.

- Chinese Proverb

1917. A loose tooth will not rest until it's pulled out.

- Bulgarian Proverb

1918. You can't end lives to save them.

- Anon

1919. Measure thrice, cut once.

- Dutch Proverb

1920. If you declare war on others, you declare war on yourself.

- Anon

1921. If we knew what it was we were doing, it would not be called research, would it?

- Albert Einstein

1922. Cynical realism is the intelligent man's best excuse for doing nothing in an intolerable situation.

- Aldous Huxley

1923. Who is curious gets old quickly.

- Chinese Proverb

1924. Reality is merely an illusion, albeit a very persistent one.

- Albert Einstein

1925. The path is made by walking.

- Dutch Proverb

1926. The way to win a war is to make certain it never starts.

- Omar Bradley

1927. If the facts don't fit the theory, change the facts.

- Albert Einstein

1928. Be a master of the mind, not mastered by the mind.

- Zen Proverb

1929. Alexander the Great....when he had conquered what was called the Eastern World...wept of more Worlds to conquer.

- Isaac Watts

1930. But if thought corrupts language, language can also corrupt thought.

- George Orwell

1931. All things can corrupt when minds are prone to evil.

- Ovid

1932. Time has no divisions to mark its passage; there is never a thunderstorm or blare of trumpets to announce the beginning of a new month. Even when a new century begins it is only we mortals who ring bells and fire off pistols.

- Thomas Mann

1933. Young wood makes a hot fire.

- Greek Proverb

1934. What's not destroyed by Time's devouring hand? Where's Troy?"

- James Bramstom

1935. The first law of dietetics seems to be if it tastes good, it's bad for you.

- Isaac Asmiov

1936. There will always be a lost dog somewhere that will prevent me from being happy.

- La Sauvage
(The Restless Heart)

1937. As we unweave a rainbow, it becomes less wonderful.

- Richard Dawkins

1938. Deeds are fruits, words are but leaves.

- Anon

1939. Better to go back than go wrong.

- Buddhist Proverb

1940.   Distance lends enhancement to the view.

- Zen Proverb

1941.   Don't bargain for fish which are still in the water.

- Indian Proverb

1942.   A king's child is a slave elsewhere.

- African Proverb

1943.   The only reason for time is so that everything doesn't happen at once.

- Albert Einstein

1944.   Empty bags cannot stand upright.

- Anon

1945.   Good company on the road is the shortest cut.

- Budai

1946.   It is better to be green and growing than ripe and rotten.

- Budai

1947.   The best ground bears weeds as well as flowers.

- Zen Proverb

1948.   A short cut is often a wrong cut.

- Anon

1949.   Little strokes fell great oaks.

- Buddhist Proverb

1950.   A chain is no stronger than its weakest link.

- Anon

1951.   Lost time is never found again.

- Buddhist Proverb

1952.   Many drops make a shower.

- Anon

1953.   Necessity is a hard nurse, but she raises strong children.

- English Proverb

1954.   A little body doth often harbour a great soul.

- Budai

1955.   A light purse makes a heavy heart.

- American Proverb

1956.   A little each day is much in a year.

- American Proverb

1957.   A man's intentions seldom add to his income.

- American Proverb

1958.   A poor man is better than a liar.

- English Proverb

1959.   A single penny fairly got is worth a thousand that are not.

- English Proverb

1960.   He who can no longer pause to wonder and stand rapt in awe, is as good as dead; his eyes are closed.

- Albert Einstein

1961.   Be happy while you are living for you are a long time dead.

- Scottish Proverb

1962.   Better to have than to wish.

- Anon

1963.   Hasty judgments are generally faulty.

- Buddhist Proverb

1964.   If you don't know where you're going, then the journey is never ending.

- Zen Proverb

1965.   The golden age never was the present one.

- Anon

1966.   We do not always gain by changing.

- Buddhist Proverb

1967.   He has enough who is content.

- Buddhist Proverb

1968.   For me, it is far better to grasp the universe as it really is than to persist in delusion however satisfying and reassuring.

- Carl Sagan

1969.   Advice when most needed is least heeded.

- Budai

1970.   No amount of experimentation can ever prove me right; a single experiment can prove me wrong.

- Albert Einstein

1971.   The fool wanders, the wise man travels.

- Siddhartha Gautama

1972.   The owl is the wisest of all birds, because the more it sees, the less it talks.

- African Proverb

1973.   A close friend can become a close enemy.

- Ethiopian Proverb

1974.   A man is not old until his regrets take the place of his dreams.

- Yiddish Proverb

1975.   A country can be judged by the quality of its proverbs.

- German Proverb

1976.   A courtyard common to all will be swept by none.

- Chinese Proverb

1977.   A drowning man is not troubled by rain.

- Persian Proverb

1978.   A friend's eye is a good mirror.

- Irish Proverb

1979.   A good husband is healthy and absent.

- Japanese Proverb

1980.   Never before in history has innovation offered promise of so much to so many in so short a time.

- Bill Gates

1981. A hedge between keeps friendship green.

- French Proverb

1982. A wise man changes his mind, a fool never will.

- Spanish Proverb

1983. Logic is the beginning of wisdom, not the end.

- Leonard Nimoy

1984. People always fear change. People feared electricity when it was invented, didn't they? People feared coal, they feared gas-powered engines... There will always be ignorance, and ignorance leads to fear.

- Bill Gates

1985. From a certain point onward, there is no longer any turning back. That is the point that must be reached.

- Franz Kafka

1986. Some people die at 25 and aren't buried until 75.

- Benjamin Franklin

1987. I have no special talent. I am only passionately curious.

- Albert Einstein

1988. Those that know, do. Those that understand, teach.

- Aristotle

1989. I had rather excel others in the knowledge of what is excellent, than in the extent of my power and dominion.

- Alexander the Great

1990. Hope is a good breakfast, but it is a bad supper.

- Francis Bacon

1991. Leave no stone unturned.

- Euripides

1992. It is not necessary that you leave the house. Remain at your table and listen. Do not even listen, only wait. Do not even wait, be wholly still and alone. The world will present itself to you for its unmasking, it can do no other, in ecstasy it will writhe at your feet.

- Franz Kafka

1993.　The root of all superstition is that men observe when a thing hits, but not when it misses.

- Francis Bacon

1994.　He that can have patience can have what he will.
- Benjamin Franklin

1995.　It's fine to celebrate success but it is more important to head the lessons of failure.

- Bill Gates

1996.　Love is a better teacher than duty.

- Albert Einstein

1997.　Nothing has more strength than dire necessity.

- Euripides

1998.　A man can be destroyed but not defeated.

- Ernest Hemingway

1999.　It is not more vacation we need – it is more vocation.
- Eleanor Roosevelt

2000.　Even the mightiest ant will be crushed by the frailest of men.

- Anon

2001.　Remember always that you not only have the right to be an individual, you have an obligation to be one.

- Eleanor Roosevelt

2002.　People need hard times and oppression to develop psychic muscles.

- Emily Dickinson

2003.　To love is so startling, it leaves little time for anything else.
- Emily Dickinson

2004.　As for accomplishments, I just did what I had to do as things came along.

- Eleanor Roosevelt

2005.　You cannot open a book without learning.

- Confucius

2006.   A gentleman would be ashamed should his deed not match
his words.

- Confucius

2007.   The worst men often give the best advice.

- Francis Bacon

2008.   He that thinks himself the happiest man is really so; but he
that thinks himself the wisest is generally the greatest fool.

- Francis Bacon

2009.   Only the wisest and stupidest of men never change.

- Kong Qiu

2010.   When anger rises, think of the consequences.

- Kong Qiu

2011.   Extinction is the rule. Survival is the exception.

- Carl Sagan

2012.   The superior man is distressed by the limitations of his
ability; he is not distressed by the fact that men do not recognize the
ability that he has.

- Anon

2013.   The faults of a superior person are like the sun and moon.
They have their faults, and everyone sees them; they change and
everyone looks up to them.

- Chinese Proverb

2014.   Truth is so rare that it is delightful to tell it.

- Emily Dickinson

2015.   When life is too easy for us, we must be aware or we may not
be ready to meet the blows which sooner or later come to everyone.

- Eleanor Roosevelt

2016.   But the fact that some geniuses were laughed at does not
imply that all who are laughed at are geniuses. They laughed at
Columbus, they laughed at the Wright Brothers. But they also
laughed at Bozo the Clown.

- Carl Sagan

2017.	He that rises late must trot all day.

- Benjamin Franklin

2018.	Old age, believe me, is a good and pleasant thing. It is true you are gently shouldered off the stage, but then you are given such a comfortable front stall as spectator.

- Confucius

2019.	Wars are caused by undefended wealth.

- Ernest Hemingway

2020.	Association with human beings lures one into self-observation.

- Franz Kafka

2021.	There's no one thing that is true. They're all true.

- Ernest Hemingway

2022.	Houses are built to live in, and not to look on: therefore, let use be preferred before uniformity.

- Francis Bacon

2023.	There are three things extremely hard: steel, a diamond, and to know one's self.

- Benjamin Franklin

2024.	Wars are not paid for in wartime, the bill comes later.

- Anon

2025.	When in doubt, don't.

- American Proverb

2026.	Before you start some work, always ask yourself three questions – Why am I doing it, what the results might be and Will I be successful?

- Chanakya

2027.	We live in a society exquisitely dependent on science and technology, in which hardly anyone knows anything about science and technology.

- Carl Sagan

2028.　He that displays too often his wife and his wallet is in danger of having both of them borrowed.

- English Proverb

2029.　The discontented man finds no easy chair.

- Benjamin Franklin

2030.　Young people are fitter to invent than to judge; fitter for execution than for counsel; and more fit for new projects than for settled business.

- Francis Bacon

2031.　Imagination will often carry us to worlds that never were. But without it, we go nowhere.

- Carl Sagan

2032.　Intellectuals solve problems, geniuses prevent them.

- Albert Einstein

2033.　The universe seems neither benign nor hostile, merely indifferent.

- Carl Sagan

2034.　We still do not know one thousandth of one percent of what nature has revealed to us.

- Albert Einstein

2035.　Who questions much shall learn much.

- Francis Bacon

2036.　I think that somehow, we learn who we really are and then live with that decision.

- Eleanor Roosevelt

2037.　For small creatures such as we, the vastness is bearable only through love.

- Carl Sagan

2038.　In all our contacts, it is probably the sense of being really needed and wanted which gives us the greatest satisfaction and creates the most lasting bond.

- Anon

2039.   Even the loose cannon hits the target every once in a while.
- American Proverb

2040.   Science is a way of thinking much more than it is a body of knowledge.
- Carl Sagan

2041.   When will our conscience grow so tender that we will act to prevent human misery rather than avenge it?
- Anon

2042.   Education is the best friend.
- Chanakya

2043.   All mankind is divided into three classes: those that are immoveable, those that are moveable, and those that move.
- Benjamin Franklin

2044.   If we do not maintain justice, justice will not maintain us.
- Francis Bacon

2045.   Never do anything against conscience, even if the state demands it.
- Albert Einstein

2046.   Occurrences in this domain are beyond the reach of exact prediction because of the variety of factors in operation, not because of any lack of order in nature.
- Albert Einstein

2047.   I very rarely think in words at all. A thought comes, and I may try to express it in words afterwards.
- Albert Einstein

2048.   There is no logical way to the discovery of these elemental laws. There is only the way of intuition, which is helped by a feeling for order lying behind the appearance.
- Albert Einstein

2049.   A man wrapped up in himself makes a very small bundle.
- Benjamin Franklin

2050.   There is poison in the fang of the serpent, in the mouth of the fly and in the sting of a scorpion, but the wicked man is saturated with it.

- Chanakya

2051.   At twenty years of age, the will reigns; at thirty, the wit; and at forty, the judgment.

- Benjamin Franklin

2052.   If you desire many things, many things will seem few.

- Benjamin Franklin

2053.   Don't throw stones at your neighbors if your own windows are glass.

- Benjamin Franklin

2054.   Beware the hobby that eats.

- Benjamin Franklin

2055.   Nothing doth more hurt than that cunning men pass for wise.

- Francis Bacon

2056.   Truth is so hard to tell, it sometimes needs fiction to make it plausible.

- Francis Bacon

2057.   Riches are a good hand maiden but a poor mistress.

- Francis Bacon

2058.   The fragrance of flowers spreads only in the direction of the wind. But goodness spreads in all directions.

- Chanakya

2059.   Keep company with those who uplift you.

- Epictetus

2060.   Nothing is enough for the man to whom enough is too little.

- Epicurus

2061.   Death does not concern us, because as long as we exist, death is not here. And when it does come, we no longer exist.

- Epicurus

2062.   As a single withered tree, if set aflame, causes a whole forest to burn, so does a rascal son destroy a whole family.

- Chanakya

2063.   Not what we have but what we enjoy constitutes our abundance.

- Epicurus

2064.   It is not so much our friend's help that helps us, as the confidence of their help.

- Greek Proverb

2065.   The misfortune of the wise is better than the prosperity of the fool.

- Anon

2066.   The time when most of you should withdraw into yourself is when you are forced to be in a crowd.

- Greek Proverb

2067.   The gift of fantasy has meant more to me than my talent for absorbing positive knowledge.

- Albert Einstein

2068.   Give light and the darkness will disappear of itself.
- Desiderius Erasmus

2069.   Prevention is better than cure.

- Desiderius Erasmus

2070.   I conceive that the great part of the miseries of mankind are brought upon them by false estimates they have made of the value of things.

- Benjamin Franklin

2071.   The only thing that interferes with my learning is my education.

- Albert Einstein

2072.   Fortune favors the audacious.

- Anon

2073. There are some people who live in a dream world, and there are some who face reality; and then there are those who turn one into the other.

- Desiderius Erasmus

2074. Half a truth is often a great lie.

- Benjamin Franklin

2075. Work as if you were to live a hundred years. Pray as if you were to die tomorrow.

- American Proverb

2076. A countryman between two lawyers is like a fish between two cats.

- North American Proverb

2077. It is a miracle that curiosity survives formal education.

- Albert Einstein

2078. Joy in looking and comprehending is nature's most beautiful gift.

- Albert Einstein

2079. Be careful to leave your sons well instructed rather than rich, for the hopes of the instructed are better than the wealth of the ignorant.

- Epictetus.

2080. A nail is driven out by another nail. Habit is overcome by habit.

- Desiderius Erasmus

2081. A man is born alone and dies alone.

- Chanakya

2082. The attempt to combine wisdom and power has only rarely been successful and then only for a short while.

- German Proverb

2083. He who allows oppression shares the crime.

- Dutch Proverb

2084.   In the kingdom of the blind, the one-eyed man is king.

- Desiderius Erasmus

2085.   The desire to write grows with writing.

- Dutch Proverb

2086.   No one respects a talent that is concealed.

- Dutch Proverb

2087.   Fools are without number.

- Anon

2088.   When I get a little money, I buy a book; and if any is left, I buy food and clothes.

- Desiderius Erasmus

2089.   The devil has put a penalty on all things we enjoy in life. Either we suffer in health or we suffer in soul or we get fat.

- Albert Einstein

2090.   Information is not knowledge.

- Albert Einstein

2091.   Most of the fundamental ideas of science are essentially simple, it may, as a rule, be expressed in a language comprehensible to everyone.

- Albert Einstein

2092.   Confusion of goals and perfection seems to characterize our age.

- Anon

2093.   Small is the number of people who see with their eyes and think with their minds.

- Zen Proverb

2094.   Humility is truth.

- Desiderius Erasmus

2095.   To find joy in work is to discover the fountain of youth.

- Pearl S. Buck

2096.   I do not judge, I only chronicle.

- John Singer Sargent

2097.   Having been poor is no shame, but being ashamed of it, is.
- Benjamin Franklin

2098.   If you want to improve, be content to be thought foolish and stupid.

- Epictetus

2099.   Is freedom anything else than the right to live as we wish? Nothing else.

- Epictetus

2100.   Don't underestimate your opponent, but don't overestimate them, either.

- Nancy Pelosi

2101.   Do good to your friends to keep them, to your enemies to win them.

- Chinese Proverb

2102.   Only the educated are free.

- Greek Proverb

2103.   It is easier to prevent bad habits than to break them.
- American Proverb

2104.   We should not moor a ship with one anchor, or out life with one hope.

- Epictetus

2105.   Time takes away the grief of men.

- Desiderius Erasmus

2106.   Let every man be respected and no man idolized.
- Albert Einstein

2107.   Whoever does not regard what he has as most ample wealth, he has as most ample wealth, is unhappy, though he be master of the world.

- Epictetus

2108.	What we need is more people who specialize in the impossible.

- Theodore Roethke

2109.	It is only when the rich are sick that they fully feel the impotence of wealth.

- Benjamin Franklin

2110.	Have patience. All things are difficult before they become easy.

- Saadi

2111.	The more we elaborate our means of communication, the less we communicate.

- J.B. Priestley

2112.	People are not disturbed by things, but by the view they take of them.

- Epictetus

2113.	It is not folly to live in misery, it's human.

- Dutch Proverb

2114.	No great thing is created suddenly.

- Greek Proverb

2115.	Nowadays the rage for possession has got to such a pitch that there is nothing in the realm of nature, whether sacred or profane, out of which profit cannot be squeezed.

- Desiderius Erasmus

2116.	The most disadvantageous peace is better than the most just war.

- Desiderius Erasmus

2117.	Don't give your advice before you are called upon.

- Dutch Proverb

2118.	A good portion of speaking will consist in knowing how to lie.

- Anon

2119.   A person should not be too honest. Straight trees are cut first and honest people are screwed first.

- Chanakya

2120.   What difference is there, do you think, between those in Plato's cave who can only marvel at the shadows and images of various objects, provided they are content and don't know what they miss, and the philosopher who has emerged from the cave and sees the real things?

- Greek Proverb

2121.   War is sweet to those who have not experienced it.

- Anon

2122.   Concealed talent brings no reputation.

- Anon

2123.   Difficulties are things that show a person what they are.

- Epictetus

2124.   It is impossible to begin to learn that which one thinks one already knows.

- Epictetus

2125.   The hood does not make the monk.

- Siddhartha Gautama

2126.   Beauty is a fragile gift.

- Ovid

2127.   The sharp thorn often produces delicate roses.

- Ovid

2128.   Habits change into character.

- Ovid

2129.   Keep love in your heart. A life without it is like a sunless garden when the flowers are dead.

- Oscar Wilde

2130.   We are ever striving after what is forbidden.

- Ovid

2131.   The man who has experienced shipwreck shudders even at a calm sea.

- Ovid

2132.   Men do not value a good deed unless it brings a reward.

- Ovid

2133.   Make the workmanship surpass the materials.

- Ovid

2134.   In our leisure we reveal what kind of people we are.

- Ovid

2135.   You can learn from anyone, even your enemy.

- Ovid

2136.   What is without periods of rest will not endure.

- Ovid

2137.   You can discover more about a person in an hour of play than in a year of conversation.

- Plato

2138.   Courage is knowing what not to fear.

- Plato

2139.   Good people do not need laws to tell them to act responsibly, while bad people will find a way around the laws.

- Plato

2140.   The measure of a man is what he does with power.

- Plato

2141.   There are two things a person should be angry at, what they can help, and what they cannot.

- Plato

2142.   He who is not a good servant will not be a good master.

- Plato

2143.   One cannot practice many arts with success.

- Plato

2144.	Thinking: the talking of the soul with itself.

- Plato

2145.	There is no harm in repeating good deeds.

- Plato

2146.	Poetry is nearer to vital truth than history.

- Plato

2147.	The greatest talents often lie buried out of sight.

- Plautus

2148.	Patience is the best remedy for every trouble.

- Plautus

2149.	A mouse does not rely on just one hole.

- Plautus

2150.	The day, water, sun, moon, night – I do not have to purchase these things with money.

- Plautus

2151.	Nothing is more wretched than the mind of a man conscious of guilt.

- Plautus

2152.	Keep what you have; the known evil is best.

- Plautus

2153.	Laughter is not at all a bad beginning for a friendship, and it is by far the best ending for one.

- Oscar Wilde

2154.	Good courage in a bad affair is half of the evil overcome.

- Plautus

2155.	It is well for one to know more than he says.

- Plautus

2156.	You must spend money to make money.

- Plautus

2157. He means well is useless unless he does well.

- Plautus

2158. The only certainty is that nothing is certain.

- Pliny the Elder

2159. An object in possession seldom retains the same charm that it had in pursuit.

- Pliny the Elder

2160. I think it's a mistake to ever loo for hope outside of one's self.

- Arthur Miller

2161. We grieve only for what we know has happened, but we fear all that possibly may happen.

- Pliny the Elder

2162. We cannot be wise at all moments.

- Pliny the Elder

2163. Whatever is begun in anger ends in shame.

- Benjamin Franklin

2164. To know oneself is to study oneself in action with another person.

- Bruce Lee

2165. However many holy words you read, however many you speak, what good will they do you if you do not act upon them?

- Buddha

2166. Home is where the heart is.

- Pliny the Elder

2167. Death, so called, is a thing which makes men weep, and yet a third of life passed in sleep.

- Byron

2168. Truth comes out in wine.

- Pliny the Elder

2169. From the end spring new beginnings.

2170.   The depth of darkness to which you can descend and still live is an exact measure of the height to which you can aspire to reach.

- Pliny the Elder

2171.   Wealth possesses mankind rather than mankind possesses wealth.

- Pliny the Elder

2172.   It is generally much more shameful to lose a good reputation than never to have acquired it.

- Pliny the Elder

2173.   To be yourself in a world that is constantly trying to make you something else is the greatest accomplishment.

- Ralph Waldo Emerson

2174.   For everything you have missed, you have gained something else, and for everything you gain, you lose something else.

- Ralph Waldo Emerson

2175.   Everything that irritates us about others can lead us to an understanding of ourselves.

- Carl Jung

2176.   Absence of evidence is not evidence of absence.

- Carl Sagan

2177.   Nothing great was ever achieved without enthusiasm.

- Ralph Waldo Emerson

2178.   Shallow men believe in luck. Strong men believe in cause and effect.

- Ralph Waldo Emerson

2179.   We gain the strength of the temptation we resist.

- Ralph Waldo Emerson

2180.   A man is great deeds, not by birth.

- Chankya

2181.   Never share your secrets with anybody. It will destroy you.

2182. Age doesn't mean a thing. The best tunes are played on the oldest fiddles.

- Ralph Waldo Emerson

2183. The reward of a thing well done is having done it.

- Ralph Waldo Emerson

2184. Win as if you were used to it, lose as if you enjoyed it for a change.

- Ralph Waldo Emerson

2185. Aim above the mark to hit the mark.

- Ralph Waldo Emerson

2186. Knowledge is knowing that we cannot know.

- Ralph Waldo Emerson

2187. If you would be a real seeker after truth, it is necessary that at least once in your life, you doubt all things, as far as possible.

- Rene Descartes

2188. Whenever anyone has offended me, I try to raise my soul so high that the offense cannot reach it.

- Rene Descartes

2189. The human heart has hidden treasures, In secret kept, in silence sealed; The thoughts, the hopes, the dreams, the pleasures, Whose charms were broken if revealed.

- Charlotte Bronte

2190. The first precept was never to accept a thing as true until I knew it as such without a single doubt.

- Rene Descartes

2191. One cannot conceive anything so strange and so implausible that is has not already been said by one philosopher.

- Rene Descartes

2192. Illusory joy is often worth more than genuine sorrow.

- Rene Descartes

2193.	Each problem that I solved became a rule, which served afterwards to solve other problems.

- Rene Descartes

2194.	I hope that posterity will judge me kindly, not only at to the things which I have explained, but also to those which I have intentionally omitted so as to leave to others the pleasure of discovery.

- Rene Descartes

2195.	Everything is self-evident.

- Rene Descartes

2196.	The two operations of our understanding, intuition and education, on which alone we have said we must rely in the acquisition of knowledge.

- Rene Descartes

2197.	Teachers who help to open young minds perform a duty which is as near sacred as I will admit.

- Richard Dawkins

2198.	Metaphors are fine if they aid understanding, but sometimes they get in the way.

- Richard Dawkins

2199.	The universe doesn't owe us condolence or consolation; it doesn't owe us a nice warm feeling inside.

- Richard Dawkins

2200.	I accept that there may be things far grander and more incomprehensible than we can possibly imagine.

- Richard Dawkins

2201.	Words raise consciousness.

- Richard Dawkins

2202.	How can you take seriously someone who likes to believe something because he finds it "comforting?"

- Richard Dawkins

2203.	The solution often turns out more beautiful than the puzzle.

- Richard Dawkins
2204.   Never be satisfied with not understanding the world.

- Richard Dawkins

2205.   A delusion is something people believe in despite a total lack of evidence.

- Richard Dawkins

2206.   There is something infantile in the presumption that somebody else has a responsibility to give your life meaning and point... The truly adult view, by contrast, is that our life is as meaningful, as full and as wonderful as we choose to make it.

- Richard Dawkins

2207.   Don't judge each day by the harvest you reap but by the seeds that you plant.

- Robert Lewis Stevenson

2208.   A friend is a gift you give yourself.

- Robert Lewis Stevenson

2209.   Compromise is the cheapest lawyer.

- Robert Lewis Stevenson

2210.   I travel not to go anywhere, but to go.

- Robert Lewis Stevenson

2211.   Give him enough rope and he will hang himself.

- Charlotte Bronte

2212.   Life is not a matter of holding good cards, but of playing a poor hand well.

- Robert Lewis Stevenson

2213.   Our life is not to succeed, but to continue to fail in good spirits.

- Robert Lewis Stevenson

2214.   Everybody, soon or later, sits down to a banquet of consequences.

- Robert Lewis Stevenson

2215.   The cruelest lies are often told in silence.

- Robert Lewis Stevenson

2216.   Keep your fears to yourself, but share your courage with others.

- Robert Lewis Stevenson

2217.   The Devil can sometimes do a very gentlemanly thing.

- Robert Lewis Stevenson

2218.   Intelligence without ambition is a bird without wings.

- Salvador Dali

2219.   Drawing is the honesty of the art. There is no possibility of cheating. It is either good or bad.

- Salvador Dali

2220.   Have no fear of perfection – you'll never reach it.

- Salvador Dali

2221.   I don't do drugs. I am drugs.

- Salvador Dali

2222.   I am no bird; and no net ensnares me; I am a free human being with an independent will.

- Charlotte Bronte

2223.   There is only one difference between a madman and me. The madman thinks he is sane. I know I am mad.

- Salvador Dali

2224.   What is a television apparatus to man, who has only to shut his eyes to see the most inaccessible regions of the seen and the never seen.

- Salvador Dali

2225.   The difference between false memories and true ones is the same as for jewels; it is always the false ones that look the most real.

- Salvador Dali

2226.   Surrealism is destructive, but it destroys only what it considers to be shackles limiting our vision.

- Salvador Dali

2227. Money is a glory.

- Salvador Dali

2228. Don't bother to be modern.

- Salvador Dali

2229. We are all born mad. Some remain so.

- Samuel Beckett

2230. You're on Earth. There is no cure for that.

- Samuel Beckett

2231. Words are all we have.

- Samuel Beckett

2232. To find a form that accommodates the mess, that is the task of the artist now.

- Samuel Beckett

2233. What do I know of man's destiny? I could tell you more about radishes.

- Samuel Beckett

2234. The tears of the world are a constant quality. For each one who begins to weep, somewhere else another stops. The same is true of the laugh.

- Samuel Beckett

2235. It is right that he too should have his little chronicle, his memories, his reason, and be able to recognize the good in the bad, the bad in the worst, and so grow gently old down all unchanging days, and die one day like any other day, only shorter.

- Samuel Beckett

2236. Habit is a great deadener.

- Samuel Beckett

2237. Poets are the sense, philosophers the intelligence of humanity.

- Samuel Beckett

2238. Everywhere I go I find that a poet has been there before me.

- Sigmund Freud

2239. Every word is like an unnecessary stain on silence and nothingness.

- Samuel Beckett

2240. He that has eyes to see and ears to hear may convince himself that no mortal can keep a secret. If his lips are silent, he chatters with his fingertips; betrayal oozes out of him at every pore.

- Sigmund Freud

2241. The conscious mind may be compared to a fountain playing in the sun and falling back into the great subterranean pool of subconscious from which it rises.

- Sigmund Freud

2242. Analysis does not set out to make pathological reactions impossible, but to give the patient' ego freedom to decide one way or another.

- Sigmund Freud

2243. A man should not strive to eliminate his complexes but to get into accord with them; they are legitimately what directs his conduct in the world.

- Sigmund Freud

2244. If youth knew; if age could.

- Sigmund Freud

2245. Most people do not really want freedom, because freedom involves responsibility, and most people are frightened of responsibility.

- Sigmund Freud

2246. Love and work are the cornerstones of our humanness.

- Sigmund Freud

2247. Illusions commend themselves to us because they save us pain and allows us to enjoy pleasure instead. We must therefore accept it without complaint when they sometimes collide with a bit of reality against which they are dashed to pieces.

- Sigmund Freud

2248. He does not believe that does not live according to his belief.

- Sigmund Freud

2249. Beware the barrenness of a busy life.

- Socrates

2250. If you get a good wife, you'll become happy; if you get a bad one, you'll become a philosopher.

- Socrates

2251. Look twice before you leap.

- Charlotte Bronte

2252. Be as you wish to seem.

- Socrates

2253. Wisdom begins in wonder.

- Socrates

2254. True wisdom comes to each of us when we realize how little we understand about life, ourselves and the world around us.

- Socrates

2255. Worthless people live only to eat and drink; people of worth eat and drink only to live.

- Socrates

2256. Let him that would move the world, first move himself.

- Socrates

2257. The unexamined life is not worth living.

- Socrates

2258. An honest man is always a child.

- Socrates

2259. If a man is proud of his wealth, he should not be praised until it is known how he employs it.

- Socrates

2260. Who seeks shall find.

- Sophocles

2261.   Rather fail with honor than succeed by fraud.

- Sophocles

2262.   Trust dies, but mistrust blossoms.

- Sophocles

2263.   If you were to offer a thirsty man all wisdom, you would not please him more than if you gave him a drink.

- Sophocles

2264.   Children are the anchors that hold mother to life.

- Sophocles

2265.   Quick decisions are unsafe decisions.

- Sophocles

2266.   Success is dependent on effort.

- Sophocles

2267.   Better to be without logic than without feeling.

- Charlotte Bronte

2268.   Men should pledge themselves to nothing; for reflection makes a liar to their resolution.

- Sophocles

2269.   No speech can stain what is noble by nature.

- Sophocles

2270.   Old age and the passage of time teach all things.

- Sophocles

2271.   Taste every fruit of every tree in the garden at least once. It is an insult to creation not to experience it fully. Temperance is wickedness.

- Stephen Fry

2272.   You can't reason yourself back into cheerfulness any more than you can reason yourself into an extra six inches in height.

- Stephen Fry

2273.   We admire what we are not.

- Stephen Fry

2274.   I think we have all experienced passion that is not in any sense reasonable.

- Stephen Fry

2275.   Having great intellect is no path to being happy.

- Stephen Fry

2276.   I am a lover of truth, a worshipper of freedom, a celebrant at the altar of language and purity and tolerance.

- Stephen Fry

2277.   Incuriosity is the oddest and most foolish failing there is.

- Stephen Fry

2278.   Life is so constructed, that the event does no, cannot, will not, match the expectation.

- Charlotte Bronte

2279.   One technology doesn't replace another, it complements. Books are no more threatened by Kindle than stairs by elevators.

- Stephen Fry

2280.   Life, that can shower you with so much splendor, is unremittingly cruel to those who have given up.

- Stephen Fry

2281.   There is nothing so self-righteous nor so right as an adolescent imagination.

- Stephen Fry

2282.   In my opinion, there is no aspect of reality beyond the reach of the human mind.

- Stephen Hawking

2283.   No one undertakes research in physics with the intention of winning a prize. It is the joy of discovering something no one knew before.

- Stephen Hawking

2284.   Scientists have become the bearers of the torch of discovery in our quest for knowledge.

- Stephen Hawking

2285.	My goal is simple. It is a complete understanding of the universe, why it is as and why it exists at all.

- Stephen Hawking

2286.	People who boast about their IQ are losers.

- Stephen Hawking

2287.	I'm not afraid of death, but I'm in no hurry to die.

- Stephen Hawking

2288.	Exploration by real people inspire us.

- Stephen Hawking

2289.	Quite people have the loudest minds.

- Stephen Hawking

2290.	We are just an advanced breed of monkeys on a minor planet of a very average star. But we can understand the Universe. That makes us something very special.

- Stephen Hawking

2291.	My expectations were reduced to zero when I was 21 after I was diagnosed with motor-neurons disease. Everything since then has been a bonus.

- Stephen Hawking

2292.	Innovation distinguishes between a leader and a follower.

- Steve Jobs

2293.	Everyone here has the sense that right now is one of those moments when we are influencing the future.

- Steve Jobs

2294.	My favorite things in life don't cost any money.

- Steve Jobs

2295.	Some people aren't used to an environment where excellence is expected.

- Steve Jobs

2296.	Things don't have to change the world to be important.

2297. Sometimes when you innovate, you make mistakes. It is best to admit them quickly, and get on with improving your other innovations.

- Steve Jobs

2298. I want to be the best, not the biggest.

- Steve Jobs

2299. Older people ask, "What is it?" but the children ask, "What can I do with it?"

- Steve Jobs

2300. It's not a faith in technology. It's faith in people.

- Steve Jobs

2301. I tried to intersect technology and art.

- Steve Jobs

2302. If you know the enemy and know yourself, you need not fear a hundred battles.

- Sun Tzu

2303. Regard your soldiers as your children, and they will follow you into the deepest valleys; look on them as your own beloved sons, and they will stand by you even unto death.

- Sun Tzu

2304. The opportunity to secure ourselves against defeat lies in our own hands, but the opportunity of defeating the enemy is provided by the enemy himself.

- Sun Tzu

2305. He who knows when he can fight and when he cannot, will be victorious.

- Sun Tzu

2306. The quality of decision is like the well-timed swoop of a falcon which enables it to strike and destroy its victim.

- Sun Tzu

2307. Pretend inferiority and encourage his arrogance.

2308.   He who is prudent and lies in wait for an enemy who is not will win.

- Sun Tzu

2309.   Be extremely subtle, even to the point of formlessness. Be extremely mysterious, even to the point of soundlessness. Thereby you can be the director of the opponent's fate.

- Sun Tzu

2310.   Do not attack the enemy, attack the enemy's strategy.

- Sun Tzu

2311.   A day wasted on others is not wasted on oneself.

- Charles Dickens

2312.   There is no instance of a nation benefitting from a prolonged warfare.

- Sun Tzu

2313.   If you expect nothing from anybody, you're never disappointed.

- Sylvia Plath

2314.   The worst enemy to creativity is self-doubt.

- Sylvia Plath

2315.   I shut my eyes and all the world drops dead; I lift my eyes and all is born again.

- Sylvia Plath

2316.   If neurotic is wanting two mutually exclusive things at one and the same time, then I'm neurotic as hell. I'll be flying back and forth between one mutually exclusive thing and another for the rest of my days.

- Sylvia Plath

2317.   If I have not the power to out myself in the place of other people, but must be continually burrowing inward, I shall never be the magnanimous creative person I wish to be. Yet I am hypnotized by the workings of the individual alone, and am continually using myself as a specimen.

2318.   Perhaps when we find ourselves wanting everything, it is because we are dangerously close to wanting nothing.

- Sylvia Plath

2319.   Wear your heart on your skin in this life.

- Sylvia Plath

2320.   What I want back is what I was.

- Sylvia Plath

2321.   What a man is is an arrow into the future, and what a woman is is the place the arrow shoots off from.

- Sylvia Plath

2322.   Is there no way out of the mind?

- Sylvia Plath

2323.   For time is the longest distance between two places.

- Tennessee Williams

2324.   We have to distrust each other. It is our only defense against betrayal.

- Tennessee Williams

2325.   There is a time for departure even when there's no certain place to go.

- Tennessee Williams

2326.   Luck is believing you're lucky.

- Tennessee Williams

2327.   Life is an unanswered question, but let's still believe in the importance of that question.

- Tennessee Williams

2328.   We are all sentenced to solitary confinement inside our own skins, for life.

- Tennessee Williams

2329.   Success is blocked by concentrating on it.

- Tennessee Williams

2330. Success is shy – it wont come out while you're watching.
- Tennessee Williams

2331. We all live in a house on fire, no fire department to call; no way out, just the upstairs window to look out of while the fire burns the house with us trapped, locked in it.
- Tennessee Williams

2332. I have always depended on the kindness of strangers.
- Tennessee Williams

2333. The things that we love tell us what we are.
- Thomas Acquinas

2334. To one who has faith, no explanation is necessary. To one without faith, no explanation is possible.
- Thomas Acquinas

2335. Men cannot live without joy, therefore when he is deprived of joys, it is necessary that he become addicted to carnal pleasures.
- Thomas Acquinas

2336. If the highest aim of a captain were to preserve his ship, he would keep it in port forever.
- Thomas Acquinas

2337. Without friends, even the most agreeable pursuits become tedious.
- Thomas Acquinas

2338. Man should not consider his material possession his own, but as common to all, so as to share them without hesitation when others are in need.
- Thomas Acquinas

2339. Good can exist without evil but evil cannot exist without good.
- Thomas Acquinas

2340. Not everything that is more difficult is more meritorious.
- Thomas Acquinas

2341.   We can't have full knowledge all at once.

- Thomas Acquinas

2342.   Love takes up where knowledge leaves off.

- Thomas Acquinas

2343.   The most certain way to succeed is always to try just one more time.

- Thomas Edison

2344.   I love fool's experiments. I am always making them.

- Charles Darwin

2345.   Opportunity is missed by most people because it is dressed in overalls and looks like work.

- Thomas Edison

2346.   There's a better way to do it, find it.

- Thomas Edison

2347.   To invent, you need a good imagination and a pile of junk.

- Thomas Edison

2348.   I have friends in overalls whose friendship I would not swap for the favor of the kings of the world.

- Thomas Edison

2349.   I never did a day's work in my life. It was all fun.

- Thomas Edison

2350.   I never did anything by accident, they came by work.

- Thomas Edison

2351.   The value of an idea lies in the using of it.

- Thomas Edison

2352.   To have a great idea, have a lot of them.

- Thomas Edison

2353.   The chief function of the body is to carry the brain around.

- Thomas Edison

2354.   Nothing can stop the hero, nothing can help the fool.

- Thomas Jefferson

2355.   In matters of style, swim with the current; in matters of principle, stand like a rock.

- Thomas Jefferson

2356.   I like the dreams of the future better than the history of the past.

- Thomas Jefferson

2357.   Banks are more dangerous than armies.

- Thomas Jefferson

2358.   Do not bite at the bait of pleasure, till you know there is no hook beneath it.

- Thomas Jefferson

2359.   Better to have no ideas than false ones.

- Thomas Jefferson

2360.   It does me no injury for my neighbor to say there are twenty god or no God.

- Thomas Jefferson

2361.   One travels more useful when alone, because he reflects more.

- Thomas Jefferson

2362.   One loves to possess arms, though they hope never to have occasion for them.

- Thomas Jefferson

2363.   Whenever you do a thing, act as if all the world were watching.

- Thomas Jefferson

2364.   We shall not cease from exploration, and the end of all our exploring will be to arrive where we started and know the place for the first time.

- T.S. Eliot

2365. Only those who will risk going too far can possibly find out how far one can go.

- T.S. Eliot

2366. If you aren't in over your head, how do you know how tall you are?

- T.S. Eliot

2367. Where is the knowledge we have lost in information?

- T.S. Eliot

2368. Poetry is not a turning loose of emotion, but an escape from emotion.

- T.S. Eliot

2369. Only those who have personality and emotions know what it means to want to escape from these things.

- T.S. Eliot

2370. This is the way the world ends, not with a bang, but a whimper.

- T.S. Eliot

2371. Half of the harm that is done in this world is due to people who want to feel important. They don't mean to do harm. But the harm does not interest them.

- T.S. Eliot

2372. Deliver me from the man of excellent intention and impure heart: for the heart is deceitful above all things, and desperately wicked.

- T.S. Eliot

2373. Anxiety is the hand maiden of creativity.

- T.S. Eliot

2374. Great things are done by a series of small things brought together.

- Vincent Van Gogh

2375. You can't get up until you fall.

- Vincent Van Gogh

2376.   I dream of painting and then I paint my dream.
                                        -   Vincent Van Gogh

2377.   What would life be if we had no courage to attempt anything.
                                        -   Vincent Van Gogh

2378.   Poetry surrounds us everywhere, but putting it on paper is not so easy as looking at it.
                                        -   Vincent Van Gogh

2379.   Conscience is a man's compass.
                                        -   Vincent Van Gogh

2380.   There may be a great fire in our hearts, yet no one ever comes to warm himself at it, and the passerby's see only a wisp of smoke.
                                        -   Vincent Van Gogh

2381.   I wish they would only take me as I am.
                                        -   Vincent Van Gogh

2382.   I see drawings and pictures in the poorest of huts and the dirtiest of corners.
                                        -   Vincent Van Gogh

2383.   A good picture is equivalent to a good deed.
                                        -   Vincent Van Gogh

2384.   It never troubles the wolf how many the sheep may be.
                                        -   Virgil

2385.   They succeed because they think they can.
                                        -   Virgil

2386.   The sweetest hours fly fastest.
                                        -   Virgil

2387.   I fear those who bring gifts.
                                        -   Virgil

2388.   Endure the present and watch for better things.
                                        -   Virgil

2389. I try to avoid looking forward or backward, and try to keeping looking upward.

- Charlotte Bronte

2390. It is easy to go down into Hell: but to climb back again, to retrace one's steps to the upper air – there's the rub.

- Virgil

2391. Trust not too much to appearances.

- Virgil

2392. Each of us bears his own Hell.

- Virgil

2393. The world cares very little what you know but you are able to do counts.

- Virgil

2394. Rage supplies enemies with weapons.

- Virgil

2395. It is difficult to free fools from the chains they revere.

- Voltaire

2396. The progress of rivers to the ocean is not so rapid as that of man to error.

- Voltaire

2397. Judge a man by his questions rather than his answers.

- Voltaire

2398. Is there anyone so wise as to learn by the experience of others?

- Voltaire

2399. What is tolerance? It is the consequence of humanity. We are all formed of frailty, let us pardon reciprocally each other's folly – that is the first law of nature.

- Voltaire

2400. Every man is guilty of all the good he did not do.

- Voltaire

2401.   To succeed in the world it is not enough to be stupid, you must also be well-mannered.

- Voltaire

2402.   Love is a canvas furnished by nature and embroidered by imagination.

- Voltaire

2403.   It is vain for the coward to flee; death follows close behind; it is only by defying it that the brave escape.

- Voltaire

2404.   A witty saying proves nothing.

- Voltaire

2405.   If you are cast in a different mold to the majority, it is no merit of yours; Nature did it.

- Charlotte Bronte

2406.   Men judge us by the success of our efforts. Good looks at the efforts themselves.

- Charlotte Bronte

2407.   It is vain to say human beings out to be satisfied with tranquility; they must have action; and they will make it if they cannot find it.

- Charlotte Bronte

2408.   It's fun to do the impossible.

- Walt Disney

2409.   Quit talking and begin doing.

- Walt Disney

2410.   A kick in the teeth may be the best thing in the world. All the adversity I've had in my life, all my troubles and obstacles, have strengthened me.

- Walt Disney

2411.   I only hope that we don't lose sight of one thing – that it was all started by a mouse.

- Walt Disney

2412.   Of all of our inventions for mass communication, pictures still speak the most universally understood language.

- Walt Disney

2413.   Time and conditions change so rapidly that we must keep our aim constantly focused on the future.

- Walt Disney

2414.   When you believe in a thing, believe in it unquestionably.

- Walt Disney

2415.   Mickey Mouse popped out of my mind onto a drawing pad 20 years ago on a train ride from Manhattan to Hollywood at a time when business fortunes of my brother Roy and myself were at lowest ebb and disaster seemed right around the corner.

- Walt Disney

2416.   Never neglect your family for business.

- Walt Disney

2417.   There is more treasure in books than in all the pirate's loot on Treasure Island.

- Walt Disney

2418.   In deep sadness, there is no place for sentimentality.
- William S. Burroughs

2419.   Your mind will answer most questions if you learn to relax and wait for the answer.

- William S. Burroughs

2420.   Sometimes paranoia's just having all the facts.
- William S. Burroughs

2421.   After one look at this planet, any visitor from space would say, "I want to see the manager."

- William S. Burroughs

2422.   The face of evil is always the face of total need.
- William S. Burroughs

2423.   Nothing is true, everything is permitted.
- William S. Burroughs

2424. The aim of education is the knowledge, not of facts, but of values.

- William S. Burroughs

2425. You must learn to exist with no religion, no country, no allies.

- William S. Burroughs

2426. We know what we are, but know not what we may be.

- William Shakespeare

2427. Artists to my mind are the real architects of change, and not the political legislators who implement change after the fact.

- William S. Burroughs

2428. Desperation is the raw material of drastic change. Only those who can leave behind everything they have ever believed in can hope to escape.

- William S. Burroughs

2429. Love all, trust a few, do wrong to none.

- William Shakespeare

2430. Better three hours too soon than a minute too late.

- William Shakespeare

2431. The course of true love never did run smooth.

- William Shakespeare

2432. God gave you one face, and you make yourself another.

- William Shakespeare

2433. A fool thinks himself to be wise, but a wise man knows himself to be a fool.

- William Shakespeare

2434. Suspicion always haunts the guilty mind.

- William Shakespeare

2435. The empty vessel makes the loudest sound.

- William Shakespeare

2436. Listen to many, speak to a few.

- William Shakespeare

2437.   What is past is prologue.

- William Shakespeare

2438.   Happiness is not something ready made. It comes from your own actions.

- Dalai Lama

2439.   Sleep is the best mediation.

- Dalai Lama

2440.   In the practice of tolerance, one's enemy is the best teacher.

- Dalai Lama

2441.   There is no need for temples, no need for complicated philosophies. My brain and my heart are my temples; my philosophy is kindness.

- Dalai Lama

2442.   Technology really increased human ability. But technology cannot produce compassion.

- Dalai Lama

2443.   We all have to live together so we might as well live together happily.

- Dalai Lama

2444.   My desire to devolve authority has nothing to do with a wish to shirk responsibility.

- Dalai Lama

2445.   I describe myself as a simple Buddhist monk. No more, no less.

- Dalai Lama

2446.   If some people have the belief or view that the Dalai Lama has some miracle power, that's totally nonsense.

- Dalai Lama

2447.   A man who dares to waste one hour of time has not discovered the value of life.

- Charles Darwin

2448.	Of course, when I say that human nature is gentle, it is not 100 percent so. Every human being has that nature, but there are many people acting against their nature, being false.

- Dalai Lama

2449.	The boundaries which divide Life from Death are at best, shadowy and vague. Who shall say where the one ends, and where the other begins?

- Edgar Allen Poe

2450.	We loved with a love that was more than love.

- Edgar Allen Poe

2451.	Words have no power to impress the mind without the exquisite horror of their reality.

- Edgar Allen Poe

2452.	The ninety and nine are with dreams, content but the hope of the world made anew, is the hundredth man who is grimly bent on making those dreams come true.

- Edgar Allen Poe

2453.	Deep into that darkness peering, long I stood there, wondering, fearing, doubting, dreaming dreams no mortal ever dared to dream before.

- Edgar Allen Poe

2454.	Those who dream by day are cognizant of many things that escape those who dream only at night.

- Edgar Allen Poe

2455.	Beauty of whatever kind, in its supreme development, invariably excites the sensitive soul to tears.

- Edgar Allen Poe

2456.	I have great faith in fools; self-confidence my friends call it.

- Edgar Allen Poe

2457.	All that we see or seem is but a dream within a dream.

- Edgar Allen Poe

2458.	Experience has shown, and a true philosophy will always show, that a vast, perhaps the larger portion of the truth arises from the seemingly irrelevant.

- Edgar Allen Poe

2459.	With the new day comes new strength and new thoughts.

- Eleanor Roosevelt

2460.	Great minds discuss ideas; average minds discuss events; small minds discuss people.

- Eleanor Roosevelt

2461.	Do things you think you cannot do.

- Eleanor Roosevelt

2462.	A woman is like a tea bag – you can't tell how strong she is until you put her in hot water.

- Eleanor Roosevelt

2463.	We are afraid to care too much, for fear that the other person does not care at all.

- Eleanor Roosevelt

2464.	Do what you feel to be right – for you'll be criticized anyway.

- Eleanor Roosevelt

2465.	Never allow a person to tell you no who doesn't have the power to say yes.

- Eleanor Roosevelt

2466.	It is not fair to ask of others what you are not willing to do yourself.

- Eleanor Roosevelt

2467.	I think, at a child's birth, if a mother could ask a fairy godmother to endow it with the most useful gift, that gift should be curiosity.

- Eleanor Roosevelt

2468.	I once had a rose named after me and I was very flattered. But I was not pleased to read the description in the catalogue: no good in a bed but fine up against a wall.

- Eleanor Roosevelt

2469.   I dwell in possibility.

- Emily Dickinson

2470.   Hope is the thing with feathers that perches in the soul – and sings the tunes without the words – and never stops at all.

- Emily Dickinson

2471.   If I can stop one heart from breaking, I shall not live in vain.

- Emily Dickinson

2472.   Behavior is what a man does, not what he thinks, feels, or believes.

- Emily Dickinson

2473.   Forever is composed of nows.

- Emily Dickinson

2474.   A wounded deer leaps the highest.

- Emily Dickinson

2475.   Where thou art, that is home.

- Emily Dickinson

2476.   How strange that nature does not knock, and yet does not intrude.

- Emily Dickinson

2477.   Dogs are better than human beings because they know but do not tell.

- Emily Dickinson

2478.   Old age comes on suddenly, and not gradually as is thought.

- Emily Dickinson

2479.   The best way to find out if you can trust somebody is to trust them.

- Ernest Hemingway

2480.   The world breaks everyone, and afterward, some are strong at the broken places.

- Ernest Hemingway

2481.   Never mistake motion for action.

- Ernest Hemingway

2482.   Happiness in intelligent people is the rarest thing I know.

- Ernest Hemingway

2483.   We are all apprentices in a craft where no one ever becomes a master.

- Ernest Hemingway

2484.   The only good thing that could spoil a day was people. People were always the limiters of happiness except for the very few that were as good as spring itself.

- Ernest Hemingway

2485.   There is nothing to writing. All you do is sit down at a typewriter and bleed.

- Ernest Hemingway

2486.   Every man's life ends the same way. It is only the details of how he lived and how he died that distinguish one man from another.

- Ernest Hemingway

2487.   They wrote in the old days that it is sweet and fitting to die for one's country. But in modern war, there is nothing sweet nor fitting in your dying. You will die like a god for no good reason.

- Ernest Hemingway

2488.   All things truly wicked start from innocence.

- Ernest Hemingway

2489.   Friends show their love in times of trouble, not in happiness.

- Euripides

2490.   One loyal friend is worth ten thousand relatives.

- Euripides

2491.   There is the sky which is all men's together.

- Euripides

2492.   Question everything. Learn something. Answer nothing.

- Euripides

2493. Events will take their course, it is no good of being angry at them; he is happiest who wisely turns them to the best account.
- Euripides

2494. Do not plan for ventures before finishing what's at hand.
- Euripides

2495. Ten soldiers wisely led will beat a hundred without a head.
- Euripides

2496. Talk sense to a fool and he calls you foolish.
- Euripides

2497. The good and the wise lead quiet lives.
- Euripides

2498. This is slavery, not to speak one's thought.
- Euripides

2499. The best part of beauty is that which no picture can express.
- Francis Bacon

2500. In order for the light to shine so brightly, the darkness must be present.
- Francis Bacon

2501. Knowledge is power.
- Francis Bacon

2502. Age appears to be best in four things; old wood best to burn, old wine to drink, old friends to trust, and old authors to read.
- Francis Bacon

2503. Silence is the sleep that nourishes wisdom.
- Francis Bacon

2504. I will never be an old man. To me, old age is always 15 years older than I am.
- Francis Bacon

2505. There is no comparison between that which is lost by not succeeding and that which is lost by not trying.
- Francis Bacon

2506. A bachelor's life is a fine breakfast, a flat lunch, and a miserable dinner.

- Francis Bacon

2507. Reading maketh a full man; conference a ready man; and writing an exact man.

- Francis Bacon

2508. The job of the artist is always to deepen the mystery.

- Francis Bacon

2509. By believing passionately in something still does not exist, we create it. The nonexistent is whatever we have not sufficiently desired.

- Franz Kafka

2510. Anyone who keeps the ability to see beauty never grows old.

- Franz Kafka

2511. The pain of parting is nothing to the joy of meeting again.

- Charles Dickens

2512. I cannot force myself to use drugs to cheat on my loneliness.

- Franz Kafka

2513. The thornbush is the old obstacle in the road. It must catch fire if you want to go further.

- Franz Kafka

2514. A stair not worn hollow by footsteps is, regarded from its own point of view, only a boring something made of wood.

- Franz Kafka

2515. In argument, similes are like songs in love; they describe much, but prove nothing.

- Franz Kafka

2516. The spirit becomes free only when it ceases to be a support.

- Franz Kafka

2517. One tells as few lies as possible only by telling as few lies as possible, and not by having the least possible opportunity to do so.

- Franz Kafka

2518.   A book must be the ax for the frozen sea within us.

- Franz Kafka

2519.   Youth is happy because it has the ability to see beauty. Anyone who keeps the ability to see beauty never grows old.

- Franz Kafka

2520.   We love life, not because we are used to living but because we are used to loving.

- Friedrich Nietzsche

2521.   Whoever fights monsters should to it that in the process, he does not become a monster. And if you gaze long enough into an abyss, the abyss will gaze back into you.

- Friedrich Nietzsche

2522.   The individual has always had to struggle to keep from being overwhelmed by the tribe. If you try it, you will be lonely often, and sometimes frightened. But no price is too high to pay for the privilege of owning yourself.

- Friedrich Nietzsche

2523.   On the mountains of truth, you can never climb in vain; either you will reach a point higher up today, or you will be training your powers so that you will be able to climb higher tomorrow.

- Friedrich Nietzsche

2524.   All things are subject to interpretation, whichever interpretation prevails at a given time is a function of power and not truth.

- Friedrich Nietzsche

2525.   He who would learn to fly one day must first learn to stand and walk and run and climb and dance; one cannot fly into flying.

- Friedrich Nietzsche

2526.   Thoughts are the shadows of our feelings – always darker, emptier and simpler.

- Friedrich Nietzsche

2527.   To live is to suffer, to survive is to find some meaning in the suffering.

- Friedrich Nietzsche

2528.   The love of power is the demon of men.

- Friedrich Nietzsche

2529.   It is impossible to suffer without making someone pay for it; every complaint already contains revenge.

- Friedrich Nietzsche

2530.   An American monkey, after getting drunk on brandy, would never touch it again, and thus is much wiser than most men.

- Charles Darwin

2531.   Vitality shows in not only the ability to persist but the ability to start over.

- F. Scott Fitzgerald

2532.   Show me a hero and I'll write you a tragedy.

- F. Scott Fitzgerald

2533.   First you take a drink, then the drink takes a drink, then the drink takes you.

- F. Scott Fitzgerald

2534.   All good writing is swimming under water and holding your breath.

- F. Scott Fitzgerald

2535.   Forgotten is forgiven.

- F. Scott Fitzgerald

2536.   Personality is an unbroken series of successful gestures.

- F. Scott Fitzgerald

2537.   It is sadder to find the past again and find it inadequate to the present than it is to have it elude you and remain forever a harmonious conception of memory.

- F. Scott Fitzgerald

2538.   There are only the pursued, the pursuing, the busy and the tired.

- F. Scott Fitzgerald

2539.   My idea is always to reach my generation. The wise writer writes for the youth of his own generation, the critics of the next, and the schoolmasters of ever afterward.

- F. Scott Fitzgerald

2540.   Genius is the ability to put into effect what is on your mind.

- F. Scott Fitzgerald

2541.   I can never close my lips where I have opened my heart.

- Charles Dickens

2542.   Ignorance more frequently begets confidence than does knowledge: it is those who know little, and not those who know much, who so positively assert that this or that problem will never be solved by science.

- Charles Darwin

2543.   The soul is healed by being with children.

- Fyodor Dostoevsky

2544.   False facts are highly injurious to the progress of science, for they often endure long; but false views, if supported by some evidence, do little harm, for everyone takes a salutary pleasure in proving their falseness.

- Charles Darwin

2545.   How paramount the future is to the present when one is surrounded by children.

- Charles Darwin

2546.   A moral being is one who is capable of reflecting on his past actions and their motives – of approving of some and disapproving of others.

- Charles Darwin

2547.   If the misery of the poor be caused not by the laws of nature, but by our institutions, great is our sin.

- Charles Darwin

2548.   There are things which a man is afraid to tell even to himself, and every decent man has a number of such things stored away in his mind.

- Fyodor Dostoevsky

2549. Man is fond of counting his troubles, but he does not count his joys.

- Fyodor Dostoevsky

2550. There is no subject so old that something new cannot be said about it.

- Fyodor Dostoevsky

2551. Much unhappiness has come into the world because of bewilderment and things left unsaid.

- Fyodor Dostoevsky

2552. Power is given only to those who dare to lower themselves and pick it up.

- Fyodor Dostoevsky

2553. We cannot teach people anything; we can only help them discover it with themselves.

- Galileo Galilei

2554. A real gentleman, even if he loses everything he owns, must show no emotion. Money must be so far beneath a gentleman that it is hardly worth troubling about.

- Fyodor Dostoevsky

2555. To love someone means to see him as God intended him.
- Fyodor Dostoevsky

2556. The greatest happiness is to know the source of unhappiness.
- Fyodor Dostoevsky

2557. Happiness does not lie in happiness, but in the achievement of it.

- Fyodor Dostoevsky

2558. The sun, with all those planets revolving around it and dependent on it, can still ripen a bunch of grapes as if it had nothing else in the universe to do.

- Galileo Galilei

2559. All truths are easy to understand once they are discovered; the point is to discover them.

- Galileo Galilei

2560. I think that in the discussion of natural problems, we ought to begin not with the Scriptures, but with experiments and demonstrations.

- Galileo Galilei

2561. I have never met a man so ignorant that I couldn't learn something from him.

- Galileo Galilei

2562. Facts which at first seem improbably will, even on scant explanation, drop the cloak which has hidden them and stand forth in naked and simple beauty.

- Galileo Galilei

2563. Where the senses fail us, reason must step in.

- Galileo Galilei

2564. Life is not about finding yourself. Life is about creating yourself.

- George Bernard Shaw

2565. Measure what is measurable, and make measurable what is not so.

- Galileo Galilei

2566. In questions of science, the authority of a thousand is not worth the humble reasoning of a single individual.

- Galileo Galilei

2567. It is surely to souls to make heresy to believe what is proved.

- Galileo Galilei

2568. We are made wise not by the recollection of our past, but by the responsibility for our future.

- George Bernard Shaw

2569. Beware of false knowledge; it is more dangerous than ignorance.

- George Bernard Shaw

2570.   Progress is impossible without change, and those who cannot change their minds cannot change anything.

- George Bernard Shaw

2571.   A day without laughter is a day wasted.

- Charlie Chaplin

2572.   The single biggest problem in communication is the illusion that it has taken place.

- George Bernard Shaw

2573.   Patriotism is your conviction that this country is superior to all others because you were born in it.

- George Bernard Shaw

2574.   Do what must be done. This may not be happiness, but it is greatness.

- George Bernard Shaw

2575.   A happy family is but an earlier heaven.

- George Bernard Shaw

2576.   Freedom is the right to tell people what they do not want to hear.

- George Orwell

2577.   Success does not consist in never making mistakes but in never making the same one a second time.

- George Bernard Shaw

2578.   Better keep yourself clean and bright; you are the window through which you must see the world.

- George Bernard Shaw

2579.   In a time of universal deceit – telling the truth is a revolutionary act.

- George Orwell

2580.   Who controls the past controls the future. Who controls the present controls the past.

- George Orwell

2581.   Men can only be happy when they do not assume that the object of life is happiness.

- George Orwell

2582.   People sleep peaceably in their beds at night only because rough men stand ready to do violence on their behalf.

- George Orwell

2583.   Each generation imagines itself to be more intelligent than the one that went before it, and wiser than the one that comes after it.

- George Orwell

2584.   The essence of being human is that one does not seek perfection.

- George Orwell

2585.   Myths which are believed in tend to become true.

- George Orwell

2586.   Power is not a means, it is an end.

- George Orwell

2587.   Progress is not an illusion, it happens, but it is slow and invariably disappointing.

- George Orwell

2588.   The family is one of nature's masterpieces.

- George Santayana

2589.   To be interested in the changing seasons is a happier state of mind than to be hopelessly in love with spring.

- George Santayana

2590.   We must welcome the future, remembering that soon it will be the past; and we must respect the past, remembering that it was once all that was humanly possible.

- George Santayana

2591.   Never build your emotional life on the weakness of others.

- George Santayana

2592.   Wise men speak and fools decide.

2593.   To kill an error is as good a service as, and sometimes even better than, the establishing of a new truth or fact.

- Charles Darwin

2594.   It is a revenge the devil sometimes takes upon the virtuous, that he entraps them by the force of the very passion they have suppressed and think themselves superior to.

- George Santayana

2595.   Only the dead have seen the end of war.

- George Santayana

2596.   Wisdom comes by disillusionment.

- George Santayana

2597.   Sanity is a madness put to good use.

- George Santayana

2598.   A child educated only at school is an uneducated child.

- George Santayana

2599.   Liberty, when it begins to take root, is a plant of rapid growth.

- George Washington

2600.   Discipline is the soul of an army. It makes small numbers formidable.

- George Washington

2601.   True friendship is a plant of slow growth, and must undergo and withstand the shocks of adversity, before it is entitled to the appellation.

- George Washington

2602.   Labor to keep alive in your breast that little spark of celestial fire, called conscience.

- George Washington

2603.   Few men have virtue to withstand the highest bidder.

- George Washington

2604. Be courteous to all, but intimate with few, and let those few be well tried before you give them your confidence.

- George Washington

2605. Happiness and moral duty are inseparably connected.

- George Washington

2606. Guard against the impostures of pretended patriotism.

- George Washington

2607. When we assumed the Soldier, we did not lay aside the Citizen.

- George Washington

2608. Truth will ultimately prevail where there is pains to bring it to light.

- George Washington

2609. Coming together is a beginning; keeping together is progress; working together is success.

- Henry Ford

2610. Thinking is the hardest work there is, which is probably the reason why so few engage in it.

- Henry Ford

2611. My best friend is the one who brings out the best in me.

- Henry Ford

2612. Don't find fault, find a remedy.

- Henry Ford

2613. If money is your hope for independence you will never have it.

- Henry Ford

2614. Life is a series of experiences, each one of which makes us bigger, even though sometimes it is hard to realize this.

- Henry Ford

2615. This world was built to develop character.

- Henry Ford

2616.   We must learn that the setbacks and grieves which we endure help us in our marching onward.

- Henry Ford

2617.   Anyone who stops learning is old, whether at twenty or eighty. Anyone who keeps learning stays young. The greatest thing in life is to keep your mind young.

- Henry Ford

2618.   Have a heart that never hardens, and a temper that never tires, and a touch that never hurts.

- Charles Dickens

2619.   If everyone is moving forward together, then success takes care of itself.

- Henry Ford

2620.   A forest bird never wants a cage.

- Henry Ibsen

2621.   The spirit of truth and freedom – these are the pillars of society.

- Henry Ibsen

2622.   We are society's tools, neither more nor less.

- Henry Ibsen

2623.   The strongest man in the world is he who stand most alone.

- Henry Ibsen

2624.   A community is like a ship; everyone ought to be prepared to take the helm.

- Henry Ibsen

2625.   People who don't know how to keep themselves healthy ought to have the decency to get themselves buried, and not waste time about it.

- Henry Ibsen

2626.   The spectacles of experience through them you will see clearly a second time.

- Henry Ibsen

2627. Home life ceases to be free and beautiful as soon as it is founded on borrowing and debt.

- Henry Ibsen

2628. The majority is always wrong, the minority is rarely right.

- Henry Ibsen

2629. It is inexcusable for scientists to torture animals; let them make their experiments on journalists and politicians.

- Henry Ibsen

2630. It is cursed evil to any man to become as absorbed in any subject as I am.

- Charles Darwin

2631. If you feel down yesterday, stand up today.

- H.G. Wells

2632. Beauty is in the heart of the beholder.

- H.G. Wells

2633. Affliction comes to us, not to make us sad but sober; not to make us sorry but wise.

- H. G. Wells

2634. The path of the least resistance is the path of the loser.

- H.G. Wells

2635. Adapt or perish.

- H.G. Wells

2636. Our true nationality is mankind.

- H.G. Wells

2637. Heresies are experiments in man's unsatisfied search for truth.

- H.G. Wells

2638. If we don't end war, war will end us.

- H.G. Wells

2639. Human history becomes more and more a race between education and catastrophe.

2640.   Human history is the history of ideas.

- H.G. Wells

2641.   Cure sometimes, treat often, comfort always.

- Hippocrates

2642.   Healing is a matter of time, but it is sometimes also a matter of opportunity.

- Hippocrates

2643.   It is more important to know what sort of person has a disease than to know what sort of disease a person has.

- Hippocrates

2644.   Let food be thy medicine and medicine be thy food.

- Hippocrates

2645.   Natural forces within us are the true healers of disease.

- Hippocrates

2646.   Many admire, few know.

- Hippocrates

2647.   Life is short, the art long.

- Hippocrates

2648.   Everything in excess is opposed to nature.

- Hippocrates

2649.   There are in fact two things, science and opinion; the former begets knowledge, the later ignorance.

- Hippocrates

2650.   The chief virtue that language can have is clearness, and nothing detracts from it so much as the use of unfamiliar words.

- Hippocrates

2651.   There is nothing nobler or more admirable than when two people who see eye to eye keep house as man and wife, confounding their enemies and delighting their friends.

- Homer

2652.   And what he greatly thought, he nobly dared.

- Homer

2653.   The difficulty is not so great to die for a friend, as to find a friend worth dying for.

- Homer

2654.   Yet, taught by tie, my heart has learned to glow for other's good and melt at other's woe.

- Homer

2655.   The charity that is trifle to us can be precious to others.

- Homer

2656.   It is not good to have a rule of many.

- Homer

2657.   But curb thou the high spirit in thy breast, for gentle ways are best, and keep aloof from sharp contentions.

- Homer

2658.   In youth and beauty, wisdom is but rare.

- Homer

2659.   A decent boldness ever meets with friends.

- Homer

2660.   Two urns on Jove's high throne has ever stood, the source of evil one, and one of good; from thence the cup of mortal man he fills, blessings to these, to those distributes ills, to most he mingles both.

- Homer

2661.   A woman knows the face of the man she loves as a sailor knows the open sea.

- Honor de Balzac

2662.   A mother's happiness is like a beacon, lighting up the future but reflected also on the past in the guise of fond memories.

- Honor de Balzac

2663.   There is no such thing as a great talent without great willpower.

- Honor de Balzac

2664.   Love is the poetry of the senses.

- Honor de Balzac

2665.   It is easy to sit up and take notice, what is difficult is getting up and taking action.

- Honor de Balzac

2666.   Power is not revealed by striking hard or often, but by striking true.

- Honor de Balzac

2667.   Those who spend too fast never grow rich.

- Honor de Balzac

2668.   Thought is the key to all treasures.

- Honor de Balzac

2669.   Art is nature concentrated.

- Honor de Balzac

2670.   Conscience is our unerring judge until we finally stifle it.

- Honor de Balzac

2671.   Science gathers knowledge faster than society gathers wisdom.

- Isaac Asimov

2672.   The true delight is in the finding out rather than in the knowing.

- Isaac Asimov

2673.   No sensible decision can be made any longer without taking account not only the world as it is, but the world as it will be.

- Isaac Asimov

2674.   Life is pleasant. Death is peaceful. It's the transition that's troublesome.

- Isaac Asimov

2675.   Writing, to me, is simply thinking through my fingers.

- Isaac Asimov

2676.   A subtle thought that is in error may yet give rise to fruitful inquiry that can establish truths of great value.

- Isaac Asimov

2677.   I am not a speed reader. I am speed understander.

- Isaac Asimov

2678.   Violence is the last refuge of the incompetent.

- Isaac Asimov

2679.   It is not only the living who are killed in war.

- Isaac Asimov

2680.   Self-education is, I firmly believe, the only kind of education there is.

- Isaac Asimov

2681.   We build too many walls and not enough bridges.

- Isaac Newton

2682.   I do not know what I may appear to the world, but to myself I seem to have been only like a boy playing on the seashore, and diverting myself in now and then finding a smoother pebble or a prettier shell than ordinary, whilst the great ocean of truth all undiscovered before me.

- Isaac Newton

2683.   I can calculate the motion of heavenly bodies, but not the madness of people.

- Isaac Newton

2684.   Truth is ever to be found in simplicity, and not in the multiplicity and confusion of things.

- Isaac Newton

2685.   Tact is the art of making a point without making an enemy.

- Isaac Newton

2686.   Genius is patience.

-    Isaac Newton

2687.   My powers are ordinary. Only my application brings me success.

-    Isaac Newton

2688.   What goes up must come down.

-    Isaac Newton

2689.   It is the weight, not numbers of experiments that is to be regarded.

-    Isaac Newton

2690.   Plato is my friend; Aristotle is my friend, but my greatest friend is truth.

-    Isaac Newton

2691.   The whole difference between construction and creation is exactly this: that a thing constructed can only be loved after it is constructed: but a thing created is loved before it exists.

-    Charles Dickens

2692.   Mistakes are the portals of discovery.

-    James Joyce

2693.   I am tomorrow what I establish today.

-    James Joyce

2694.   My mouth is full of decayed teeth and my soul of decayed ambitions.

-    James Joyce

2695.   Better pass boldly into that other world, in the full glory of some passion, than fade and wither dismally with age.

-    James Joyce

2696.   Think you're escaping and run into yourself.

-    James Joyce

2697.   Longest way round is the shortest way home.

-    James Joyce

2698. Your battles inspired me – not the obvious battles but those that were fought and won behind your forehead.

- James Joyce

2699. The actions of men are the best interpreters of their thoughts.

- James Joyce

2700. I've put in so many enigmas and puzzles that it will keep the professors busy for centuries arguing over what I meant, and that's the only way of insuring one's immortality.

- James Joyce

2701. He found in the world without as actual what was in his world within as possible.

- James Joyce

2702. Vanity and pride are different things, though the words are often used synonymously. Pride relates more to our opinion of ourselves; vanity, to what we would have others think of us.

- Jane Austen

2703. Selfishness must always be forgiven, because there is no hope of a cure.

- Jane Austen

2704. There are people, who the more you do for them, the less they will do for themselves.

- Jane Austen

2705. Happiness in marriage is entirely a matter of chance.

- Jane Austen

2706. One man's style must not be the rule of another's.

- Jane Austen

2707. What is right cannot be done too soon.

- Jane Austen

2708. How quick come the reasons for approving what we like.

- Jane Austen

2709. Nobody minds having what is too good for them.

- Jane Austen

2710.   They are much to be pitied who have not been given a taste for nature early in life.

- Jane Austen

2711.   Those who do not complain are never pitied.

- Jane Austen

2712.   Love your enemies and pray for those who persecute you.

- Jesus Christ

2713.   Peace be with you for you all my brothers and sisters.

- Jesus Christ

2714.   If you love those who love, what credit is that to you? For even sinners love those who love them. And if you do good to those who do good to you, what credit is that to you? For even sinners do the same.

- Jesus Christ

2715.   If you want to be perfect, go, sell your possessions and give to the poor, and you will have treasure in heaven.

- Jesus Christ

2716.   Let the one among you who is without sin be the first to cast a stone.

- Jesus Christ

2717.   It is not the healthy who need a doctor, but the sick. I have not come to call the righteous, but sinners to repentance.

- Jesus Christ

2718.   Do not let your hearts be troubled. Trust in God, trust in me.

- Jesus Christ

2719.   As I have loved you, so you must love one another.

- Jesus Christ

2720.   Know that I am with you always, yes, to the end of time.

- Jesus Christ

2721.   As we express our gratitude, we must never forget that the highest appreciation is not to utter words, but to live by them.

- John F. Kennedy

2722.   Change is the law of life.

                          - John F. Kennedy

2723.   Things do not happen. Things are made to happen.

                          - John F. Kennedy

2724.   Leadership and learning are indispensable to each other.

                          - John F. Kennedy

2725.   Efforts and courage are not enough without purpose and direction.

                          - John F. Kennedy

2726.   The best road to progress is freedom's road.

                          - John F. Kennedy

2727.   We are tied to the ocean. And when we go back to the sea, whether it is to sail or to watch – we are going back from whence we came.

                          - John F. Kennedy

2728.   The goal of education is the advancement of knowledge and the dissemination of truth.

                          - John F. Kennedy

2729.   A man may die, nations may rise and fall, but an idea lives on.

                          - John F. Kennedy

2730.   The cost of freedom is always high.

                          - John F. Kennedy

2731.   There are dark shadows on the earth, but its lights are stronger in the contrast.

                          - Charles Dickens

2732.   Love is a flower, you've got to let it grow.

                          - John Lennon

2733.   Everything is clearer when you're in love.

                          - John Lennon

2734.   We've got this gift of love, but love is like a precious plant. You can't just accept it and leave it in the cupboard or just think it's going to get on by itself. You've got to keep watering it. You've got to really look after it and nurture it.

- John Lennon

2735.   When you're drowning, you don't say, "I would be incredibly pleased if someone would have the foresight to notice me drowning and come and help me." You just scream.

- John Lennon

2736.   Imagine all the people living life in peace. You may say I'm a dreamer, but I'm not the only one. I hope someday you'll join us, and the world will be as one.

- John Lennon

2737.   Reality leaves a lot to the imagination.

- John Lennon

2738.   I believe in everything until it's disproved.

- John Lennon

2739.   Everybody loves you when you're six foot in the ground.

- John Lennon

2740.   Give peace a chance.

- John Lennon

2741.   The more I see, the less I know for sure.

- John Lennon

2742.   It opens the lungs, washes the countenance, exercises the eyes, and softened down the temper, so cry away.

- Charles Dickens

2743.   I will honor Christmas in my heart, and try to keep it all the year.

- Charles Dickens

2744.   They also serve who only stand and wait.

- John Milton

2745. Gratitude bestows reverence, allowing us to encounter everyday epiphanies, those transcendent moments of awe that change forever how we experience life and the world.

- John Milton

2746. He that has light within his own clear breast, May sit in the center, and enjoys bright day; But he that hides a dark soul and foul thoughts, Benighted walks under the midday sun; Himself his own dungeon.

- John Milton

2747. Death is the golden key that opens the palace of eternity.

- John Milton

2748. Beauty is nature's brag.

- John Milton

2749. The mind is its own place and in itself, can make a Heaven of Hell, a Hell of Heaven.

- John Milton

2750. The superior man acquaints himself with many sayings of antiquity and many deeds of the past, in order to strengthen his character thereby.

- John Milton

2751. The stars, that nature hung in heaven, and filled their lamps with everlasting oil, give due light to the mislead and lonely traveler.

- John Milton

2752. Who kills a man, kills a reasonable creature, God's image, but thee who destroy a good book, kill reason its self.

- John Milton

2753. But what can war, but endless war, still breed?

- John Milton

2754. I have come to believe that a great teacher is a great artist and that there are as few as there are any other greatest artists. Teaching might even be the greatest of the arts since the medium is the human mind and spirit.

- John Steinbeck

2755.   It is a common experience that a problem difficult at night is resolved in the morning after the committee of sleep has worked on it.

- John Steinbeck

2756.   A journey is a person in itself; no two are alike.

- John Steinbeck

2757.   We do not take a trip, a trip takes us.

- John Steinbeck

2758.   You only want advice if it agrees with you.

- John Steinbeck

2759.   A sad soul can kill quicker than a germ.

- John Steinbeck

2760.   One can find so many pains when the rain is falling.

- John Steinbeck

2761.   If you're in trouble, or hurt or need – go to the poor people. They're the only ones that'll help – the only ones.

- John Steinbeck

2762.   Many a trip continues long after movement in time and space have ceased.

- John Steinbeck

2763.   The writer must believe that what he is doing is the most important thing in the world. And he must hold to this illusion even when he knows it is not true.

- John Steinbeck

2764.   Vision is the art of seeing what is invisible to others.

- Jonathan Swift

2765.   A wise man should have money in his head, but not in his heart.

- Jonathan Swift

2766.   May all you live all the days of your life.

- Jonathan Swift

2767.   The proper words in the proper places are the true definition of style.
- Jonathan Swift

2768.   When a true genius appears, you can know him by this sign; that all the dunces are in a confederacy against him.
- Jonathan Swift

2769.   Books, the children of the brain.
- Jonathan Swift

2770.   For in reason, all government without the consent of the governed is the very definition of slavery.
- Jonathan Swift

2771.   The power of fortune is confessed only by the miserable, for the happy impute all their success to prudence or merit.
- Jonathan Swift

2772.   A lie does not consist in the indirect position of words, but in the desire and intention, by false speaking, to deceive and injure your neighbor.
- Jonathan Swift

2773.   One enemy can do more hurt than ten friends can do good.
- Jonathan Swift

2774.   Find a place inside where there's joy, and the joy will burn out the pain.
- Joseph Campbell

2775.   The privilege of a lifetime is being who you are.
- Joseph Campbell

2776.   Your sacred space is where you can find yourself again and again.
- Joseph Campbell

2777.   When we quit thinking primary about ourselves and our own self-preservation, we undergo a truly heroic transformation of consciousness.
- Joseph Campbell

2778.   We must let go of the life we have planned, so as to accept the one that is waiting for us.

- Joseph Campbell

2779.   When you make the sacrifice in marriage, you're sacrificing not to each other but to unity in a relationship.

- Joseph Campbell

2780.   I don't believe people are looking for the meaning of life as much as they are looking for the experience of being alive.

- Joseph Campbell

2781.   Your life is the fruit of your own doing. You have no one to blame but yourself.

- Joseph Campbell

2782.   The goal of life is to make your heartbeat match the beat of the universe, to match your nature with Nature.

- Joseph Campbell

2783.   It is by going down into the abyss that we recover the treasure of life. Where you stumble, there lies your treasure.

- Joseph Campbell

2784.   Who knows what true loneliness is – not the convention word but the naked terror? To the lonely themselves it wears a mask. The most miserable outcast hugs some memory or some illusion.

- Joseph Conrad

2785.   Being a woman is a terribly difficult task, since it consists principally in dealing with men.

- Joseph Conrad

2786.   I take it that what all men are really after is some formula of peace.

- Joseph Conrad

2787.   Great achievements are accomplished in a bless, warm fog.

- Joseph Conrad

2788.   Face it, that's the way to get through.

- Joseph Conrad

2789.   Woe to the man whose heart has not learned while young to hope, to love – and to put its trust in life.

- Joseph Conrad

2790.   History repeats itself, but the special call of an art which has passed away is never reproduced. It is as utterly gone out of the world as the song of a destroyed wild bird.

- Joseph Conrad

2791.   In order to move others deeply we must deliberately allow ourselves to be carried away beyond the bounds of our normal sensibility.

- Joseph Conrad

2792.   Gossip is what no one claims to like, but everybody enjoys.

- Joseph Conrad

2793.   A caricature is putting the face of a joke on the body of a truth.

- Joseph Conrad

2794.   Imagine a society in which there were neither rich nor poor. What evils, afflictions, sorrows, disorders, catastrophes, disasters, tribulations, misfortunes, agonies, calamities, despair, desolation and ruin would be unknown to man.

- Jules Verne

2795.   In spite of the opinions of certain narrow-minded people, who would shut up the human race upon this globe, as within some magic circle it must never outstep, we shall one day travel to the moon, the planet, and the stars, with the same facility, rapidity, and certainty as we now make the voyage from Liverpool to New York.

- Jules Verne

2796.   However strong, however imposing a ship may appear, it is not disgraced because it flies before the tempest. A commander ought always to remember that a man's life is worth more than the mere satisfaction of his own pride. In any case, to be obstinate is blamable, and to be wilful is dangerous.

- Jules Verne

2797.   We may brave human laws, but we cannot resist natural ones.

- Jules Verne

2798.   Science is made up of mistakes, but they are mistakes which
it is useful to make, because they lead little by little to the truth.

- Jules Verne

2799.   Solitude is beyond human endurance.

- Jules Verne

2800.   You're never rich enough if you can be richer.

- Jules Verne

2801.   Trains, like time and tide, stop for no one.

- Jules Verne

2802.   Put two ships in the open sea, without wind or tide, and, at
last, they will come together. Throw two planets into space, and
they will fall one on the other. Place two enemies in the midst of a
crowd, and they will inevitably meet; it is a fatality, a question of
time; that is all.

- Jules Verne

2803.   Liberty is worth paying for.

- Jules Verne

2804.   Experience is the teacher of all things.

- Julius Caesar

2805.   It is easier to find men who will volunteer to die, than to find
those who are willing to endure pain with patience.

- Julius Caesar

2806.   No one is so brave that he is not disturbed by something
unexpected.

- Julius Caesar

2807.   It is better to create than to learn.

- Julius Caesar

2808.   What we wish, we readily believe, and what we ourselves
think, we imagine others think also.

- Julius Caesar

2809.   Men are quick to believe that which they wish to be true.

- Julius Caesar

2810. Men worry more about what they can't see than about what they can.

- Julius Caesar

2811. I rather be first in a village than second at Rome.

- Julius Caesar

2812. I love the name of honor, more than I fear death.

- Julius Caesar

2813. I came, I saw, I conquered.

- Julius Caesar

2814. Everyone thinks of changing the world, but no one thinks of changing himself.

- Leo Tolstoy

2815. The two most powerful warriors are patience and time.

- Leo Tolstoy

2816. If you want to be happy, be.

- Leo Tolstoy

2817. There is no greatness where there is no simplicity, goodness and truth.

- Leo Tolstoy

2818. I sit on a man's back, choking him and making him carry me, and yet assure myself and others that I am very sorry for him and wish to ease his lot by all possible means – except by getting off his back.

- Leo Tolstoy

2819. Joy can only be real if people look upon their life as a service and have a definite object in life outside themselves and their personal happiness.

- Leo Tolstoy

2820. All violence consists in some people forcing others, under threat of suffering or death, to do what they do not want to do.

- Leo Tolstoy

2821. Music is the shorthand of emotion.

- Leo Tolstoy

2822.   The changes in our life must come from the impossibility to live otherwise than according to the demands of our conscience not from our mental resolution to try a new form of life.

- Leo Tolstoy

2823.   Art is not a handicraft, it is the transmission of feeling the artist has experienced.

- Leo Tolstoy

2824.   Reflect upon your present blessings of which every man has many – not on your past misfortunes, of which all men have some.

- Charles Dickens

2825.   If you don't know where you are going, any road will get you there.

- Lewis Carroll

2826.   I can't go back to yesterday because I was a different person then.

- Lewis Carroll

2827.   Who in the world am I? Ah, that's the great puzzle.

- Lewis Carroll

2828.   Sometimes I've believed as many as six impossible things before breakfast.

- Lewis Carroll

2829.   She generally gave herself very good advice (thought she very seldom followed it.)

- Lewis Carroll

2830.   While the laughter of joy is in full harmony with our deeper life, the laughter of amusement should be kept apart from it. The danger is too great of thus learning to look at solemn things in a spirit of mockery, and to seek in them opportunities for exercising wit.

- Lewis Carroll

2831.   Contrariwise, if it was so, it might be; and if it were so, it would be; but as it isn't, it ain't. That's logic.

- Lewis Carroll

2832.   That's the reason they're called lessons, because they lesson from day to day.

- Lewis Carroll

2833.   All that is really worth the doing is what we do for others.

- Lewis Carroll

2834.   Everything's got a moral, if only you can find it.

- Lewis Carroll

2835.   To truly laugh, you must be able to take your pain and play with it.

- Charlie Chaplin

2836.   Nothing is permanent, not even our troubles.

- Charlie Chaplin

2837.   Music is a higher revelation than all wisdom and philosophy.

- Ludwig von Beethoven

2838.   Music is the mediator between the spiritual and the sensual life.

- Ludwig von Beethoven

2839.   Music should strike fire from the heart of man, and bring tears from the eyes of woman.

- Ludwig von Beethoven

2840.   Tones sound, and roar and storm about me until I have set them down in notes.

- Ludwig von Beethoven

2841.   A great poet is the most precious jewel of a nation.

- Ludwig von Beethoven

2842.   Don't only practice your art, but force your way into its secrets; art deserves that, for it and knowledge can raise man to the Divine.

- Ludwig von Beethoven

2843.   Art, who comprehends her? With whom can one consult concerning this great goddess?

- Ludwig von Beethoven

2844.   What you are, you are by accident of birth; what I am, I am by myself. There are and will be a thousand princes; there is only one Beethoven.

- Ludwig von Beethoven

2845.   Recommend virtue to your children; it alone, not money, can make them happy. I speak from experience.

- Ludwig von Beethoven

2846.   Music is the one incorporeal entrance into the higher world of knowledge which comprehends mankind but which mankind cannot comprehend.

- Ludwig von Beethoven

2847.   Failure is unimportant.

- Charlie Chaplin

2848.   Happiness is when what you think, what you say, and what you do are in harmony.

- Mahatma Gandhi

2849.   Only the weak never forgive.

- Mahatma Gandhi

2850.   The best way to find yourself is to lose yourself in the service of others.

- Mahatma Gandhi

2851.   Humanity is an ocean; if a few drops of the ocean are dirty, the ocean does not become dirty.

- Mahatma Gandhi

2852.   Prayer is the key of the morning and the bolt of the evening.

- Mahatma Gandhi

2853.   Non-force is the greatest force at the disposal of mankind.

- Mahatma Gandhi

2854.   Action expresses priorities.

- Mahatma Gandhi

2855. What difference does it make to the dead, the orphans, and the homeless, whether the mad destruction is wrought under the name of totalitarianism or the holy name of liberty or democracy?

- Mahatma Gandhi

2856. The moment there is suspicion about a person's motives, everything he does becomes tainted.

- Mahatma Gandhi

2857. Honest disagreement is often a good sign of progress.

- Mahatma Gandhi

2858. We think too much and feel too little.

- Charlie Chaplin

2859. Man as an individual is a genius. But men in the mass form the headless monster, a great, brutish idiot that goes where prodded.

- Charlie Chaplin

2860. Everything we hear is an opinion, not a fact.

- Marcus Aurelius

2861. The art of living is more like wrestling than dancing.

- Marcus Aurelius

2862. Within is the fountain of good, and it will ever bubble up, if thou wilt ever dig.

- Marcus Aurelius

2863. The best revenge is to be unlike him who performed the injury.

- Marcus Aurelius

2864. The soul becomes dyed with the color of its thoughts.

- Marcus Aurelius

2865. Confine yourself to the present.

- Marcus Aurelius

2866. It is not death that a man should fear, but he should fear never beginning to live.

- Marcus Aurelius

2867. Everything that happens happens as it should, and if you observe carefully, you will find this to be so.

- Marcus Aurelius

2868. A man's worth is no greater than his ambitions.

- Marcus Aurelius

2869. Each day provides its own gifts.

- Marcus Aurelius

2870. It takes courage to make a fool of yourself.

- Charlie Chaplin

2871. The secret of getting ahead is getting started.

- Mark Twain

2872. Whenever you find yourself on the side of the majority, it is time to pause and reflect.

- Mark Twain

2873. A man who lives fully is prepared to die any time.

- Mark Twain

2874. Anger is an acid that can do more harm to the vessel in which it is stored than to anything on which it is poured.

- Mark Twain

2875. You can't depend on your eyes when your imagination is out of focus.

- Mark Twain

2876. Do the right thing. It will gratify some people and astonish the rest.

- Mark Twain

2877. Many a small thing has been made large by the right kind of advertising.

- Mark Twain

2878. Don't go around saying the world owes you a living. The world owes you nothing. It was here first.

- Mark Twain

2879. When in doubt, tell the truth.

- Mark Twain

2880. It ain't what you don't know that gets you into trouble. It's what you know for sure that just ain't so.

- Mark Twain

2881. The ultimate measure of a man is not where he stands in moments of comfort and convenience, but where he stands at time of challenge and controversy.

- Martin Luther King

2882. There is some good in the worst of us and some evil in the best of us.

- Martin Luther King

2883. In the End, we will remember not the words of our enemies, but the silence of our friends.

- Martin Luther King

2884. A man can't ride you unless your back is bent.

- Martin Luther King

2885. Change does not roll in on the wheels of inevitability, but comes through continuous struggle.

- Martin Luther King

2886. I refuse to accept the view that mankind is so tragically bound to the starless midnight of racism and war that the bright daybreak of peace and brotherhood can never become a reality... I believe that unarmed truth and unconditional love will have the final word.

- Martin Luther King

2887. A genuine leader is not a searcher for consensus but a molder of consensus.

- Martin Luther King

2888. We may have all come on different ships, but we're in the same boat now.

- Martin Luther King

2889.   Nothing pains some people more than having to think.

                                              -   Martin Luther King

2890.   Injustice anywhere is a threat to justice everywhere.

                                              -   Martin Luther King

2891.   Try to be a rainbow in someone's cloud.

                                              -   Maya Angelou

2892.   I've learned that people will forget what you said, people will
         forget what you did, but people will never forget how you made
         them feel.

                                              -   Maya Angelou

2893.   My mother said I must always be intolerant of ignorance but
         understanding of illiteracy. That some people, unable to go school,
         were more educated and more intelligent than college professors.

                                              -   Maya Angelou

2894.   Nothing will work unless you do.

                                              -   Maya Angelou

2895.   You may not control all the events that happen to you, but
         you decide not to be reduced by them.

                                              -   Maya Angelou

2896.   Love recognizes no barriers. It jumps hurdles, leap fences,
         penetrates walls to arrive at its destination full of hope.

                                              -   Maya Angelou

2897.   History cannot be unlived.

                                              -   Maya Angelou

2898.   Bitter is like cancer, it eats upon the host.

                                              -   Maya Angelou

2899.   All great achievements require time.

                                              -   Maya Angelou

2900.   A wise woman wishes to be no one's enemy; a wise woman
         refuses to be anyone's victim.

                                              -   Maya Angelou

2901.　Life is a tragedy when seen in close-up, but a comedy in long-shot.

- Charlie Chaplin

2902.　What we usually consider as impossible are simply engineering problems... there's no law of physics preventing them.

- Michio Kaku

2903.　Boring exams is the well from which we draw our nourishment and energy.

- Michio Kaku

2904.　The human brain has 100 billion neurons, each neuron connected to 10,000 other neurons. Sitting om your shoulders is the most complicated object in the known universe.

- Michio Kaku

2905.　It's pointless to have a nice clean desk, because it means you're not doing anything.

- Michio Kaku

2906.　If a Martian came down to Earth and watched television, he'd come to conclusion that all world's society is based on Britney Spears and Paris Hilton. He'd be amazed that our society hasn't collapsed.

- Michio Kaku

2907.　Our grandkids will lead the lives of the gods of mythology. Zeus could think and move objects around. We'll have that power. Venus had a perfect, timeless body. We'll have that, too. Pegasus was a flying horse. We'll be able to modify life in the future.

- Michio Kaku

2908.　We have to realize that science is a double-edged sword. One edge of the sword can cut against poverty, illness, disease and give us more democracies, and democracies never war with other democracies, but the other side of the sword could give us nuclear proliferation, biogerms and even forces of darkness.

- Michio Kaku

2909.　The word "impossible" is dangerous.

- Michio Kaku

2910.	Nothing is ever 100% proven.

- Michio Kaku

2911.	You can mass-produce hardware; you cannot mass-produce software – you cannot mass-produce the human mind.

- Michio Kaku

2912.	A wise man is superior to any insults which can be put upon him and the best reply to unseemly behavior is patience and moderation.

- Moliere

2913.	The trees that are slow to grow bear the best fruit.

- Moliere

2914.	People don't mind being mean; but they never want to be ridiculous.

- Moliere

2915.	Speak to be understood.

- Moliere

2916.	I live on soup, not on fine words.

- Moliere

2917.	I prefer a pleasant vice to an annoying virtue.

- Moliere

2918.	It is not only for what we do that we are held responsible, but also for what we do not do.

- Moliere

2919.	It infuriates me to be wrong when I know when I'm right.

- Moliere

2920.	A learned fool is more than an ignorant fool.

- Moliere

2921.	Friendship is not something you learn in school. But if you haven't learned the meaning of friendship, you really haven't learned anything.

- Muhammad Ali

2922.   If you suppress grief too much, it can well redouble.

- Moliere

2923.   I hated every minute of training, but I said, "Don't quit. Suffer now and live the rest of your life as a champion."

- Muhammad Ali

2924.   Silence is golden when you can't think of a good answer.

- Muhammad Ali

2925.   Service to others is the rent you pay for your room here on Earth.

- Muhammad Ali

2926.   The fight is won or lost far away from the witnesses – behind the lies in the gym, and out there on the road, long before I dance under those lights.

- Muhammad Ali

2927.   Only a man who knows what it is like to be defeated can reach down to the bottom of his soul and come up with the extra ounce of power it takes to win when the match is even.

- Muhammad Ali

2928.   What keeps me going is goals.

- Muhammad Ali

2929.   Rivers, ponds, lakes and streams – they all have different names, but they all contain water. Just as religions do – they all contain truths.

- Muhammad Ali

2930.   It's not bragging if you can back it up.

- Muhammad Ali

2931.   I went into the business for the money, and the art grew out of it.

- Charlie Chaplin

2932.   A soldier will fight long and hard for a bit of colored ribbon.

- Napoleon Bonaparte

2933. Impossible is a word to be found only in the dictionary of fools.

- Napoleon Bonaparte

2934. I had been so great in boxing, they had to create an image like Rocky, a white image on the screen, to counteract my image in the ring. America has to have its white images, no matter it gets them. Jesus, Wonder Woman, Tarzan and Rocky.

- Muhammad Ali

2935. History is the version of past events that people have decided to agree upon.

- Napoleon Bonaparte

2936. Death is nothing, but to live defeated and inglorious is to die daily.

- Napoleon Bonaparte

2937. Victory belongs to the most persevering.

- Napoleon Bonaparte

2938. Take time to deliberate, but when the time for action has arrived, stop thinking and go in.

- Napoleon Bonaparte

2939. You must not fight too often with one enemy, or you will teach him all your art of war.

- Napoleon Bonaparte

2940. Ten people who speak make more noise than ten thousand who are silent.

- Napoleon Bonaparte

2941. There is no such thing as accident; it is fate misnamed.

- Napoleon Bonaparte

2942. I am sometimes a fox and sometimes a lion. The whole secret of government lies in knowing when to be the one or the other.

- Napoleon Bonaparte

2943. What adults primarily do in the presence of kids is unwittingly thwart the curiosity of children.

- Neil deGrasse Tyson

2944.   Science is basically an inoculation against charlatans.
- Neil deGrasse Tyson

2945.   Not enough people in this world, I think, carry a cosmic perspective with them. It could be life-changing.
- Neil deGrasse Tyson

2946.   Adults, who outnumber kids four or five to one, are in charge. We wield the resources, run the world, and completely thwart kids' creativity.
- Neil deGrasse Tyson

2947.   Everyone should have their mind blown once a day.
- Neil deGrasse Tyson

2948.   The history of exploration has never been driven by exploration. But Columbus himself was a discoverer. So was Magellan. But the people who wrote checks were not. They had other motivations.
- Neil deGrasse Tyson

2949.   Space only becomes ordinary when the frontier is no longer being breached.
- Neil deGrasse Tyson

2950.   People who are scientists today are scientists in spite of the system, typically, not because of it.
- Neil deGrasse Tyson

2951.   I'm on a crusade to get movie directors to get their science right because, more often than they believe, the science is more extraordinary than anything they can invent.
- Neil deGrasse Tyson

2952.   One of the greatest features of science is that it doesn't matter where you were born, and it doesn't matter what the beliefs systems of your parents might have been; if you perform the same experiment that someone else did, at a different time and place, you'll get the same result.
- Neil deGrasse Tyson

2953.   I am peace with God. My conflict is with Man.
- Charlie Chaplin

2954.　If I am walking with two other men, each of them will serve as my teacher. I will out the good points of the one and imitate them, and the bad points of the other and correct them in myself.

- Confucius

2955.　Experience is simply the name we give our mistakes.

- Oscar Wilde

2956.　Women are made to be loved, not understood.

- Oscar Wilde

2957.　The old believe everything, the middle-aged suspect everything, the young know everything.

- Oscar Wilde

2958.　No great artists ever sees things as they really are. If he did, he would cease to be an artist.

- Oscar Wilde

2959.　Some cause happiness wherever they go; others whenever they go.

- Oscar Wilde

2960.　All women become like their mothers. That is their tragedy. No man does. That's his.

- Oscar Wilde

2961.　Give a man a mask and he will tell the truth.

- Oscar Wilde

2962.　Consistency is the last refuge of the unimaginative.

- Oscar Wilde

2963.　Success consists of going from failure to failure without loss of enthusiasm.

- Winston Churchill

2964.　Courage is what it takes to stand up and speak; courage is also what it takes to sit down and listen.

- Winston Churchill

2965.　To improve is to change, to be perfect is to change often.

- Winston Churchill

2966.   We make a living by what we get, but we make a life by what we give.

> \- Winston Churchill

2967.   The truth is incontrovertible. Malice may attack it, ignorance may deride it, but in the end, there it is.

> \- Winston Churchill

2968.   However beautiful the strategy, you should occasionally look at the results.

> \- Winston Churchill

2969.   History will be kind to me for I intend to write it.

> \- Winston Churchill

2970.   Now this is not the end. It is not even the beginning of the end. But it is, perhaps, the end of the beginning.

> \- Winston Churchill

2971.   Truth is so precious that she should always be attended by a bodyguard of lies.

> \- Winston Churchill

2972.   It is always wise to look ahead, but difficult to look further than you can see.

> \- Winston Churchill

2973.   Life is really simple, but we insist on making it complicated.

> \- Confucius

2974.   Choose a job you love, and you will never have to work a day in your life.

> \- Confucius

2975.   When it is obvious that the goals cannot be reached, don't adjust the goals, adjust the action steps.

> \- Confucius

2976.   By three methods we may learn wisdom: First, by reflection, which noblest: Second, by imitation, which is easiest: and third by experience, which is the bitterest.

> \- Confucius

2977.   Real knowledge is to know the extent of one's ignorance.

- Confucius

2978.   The expectations of life depend upon diligence: the mechanic that would perfect his work must first sharpen his tools.

- Confucius

2979.   Never give a sword to a man who can't dance.

- Confucius

2980.   Better a diamond with a flaw than a pebble without.

- Confucius

2981.   He who learns but does not think is lost. He who thinks but does not learn is in great danger.

- Confucius

2982.   You are never too old to set another goal.

- C.S. Lewis

2983.   It may be hard for an egg to turn into a bird: it would be a jolly sight harder for it to learn to fly while remaining an egg. We are like eggs at present. And you cannot go on indefinitely being just an ordinary, decent egg. We must be hatched or go bad.

- C.S. Lewis

2984.   Integrity is doing the right thing, even when no one is watching.

- C.S. Lewis

2985.   The task of the modern educator is not to cut down jungles, but to irrigate deserts.

- C.S. Lewis

2986.   Friendship has no survival value: rather it is one of those things that give value to survival.

- C.S. Lewis

2987.   Nothing that you have not given away will ever be really yours.

- C.S. Lewis

2988. Literature adds to reality, it does not simply describe it.
                                                    - C.S. Lewis

2989. Education without values, as useful as it is seems rather to make a man a more clever devil.
                                                    - C.S. Lewis

2990. We all want progress, but if you're on the wrong road, progress means doing an about-turn and walking back to the right road: in that case, the man who turns back soonest is the most aggressive.
                                                    - C.S. Lewis

2991. What is right and what is practical are two different things."
                                                    - James Buchanan

2992. To vote is like the payment of a debt, a duty never to be neglected, if its performance is possible.
                                                    - Rutherford B. Hayes

2993. If you can't stand the heat, get out of the kitchen.
                                                    - Harry S. Truman

2994. Self-love, my liege is not so vile a sin, as self-neglecting.
                                                    - William Shakespeare

2995. Pleasure and action make the hours seem short.
                                                    - William Shakespeare

2996. With mirth and laughter let old wrinkles come.
                                                    - William Shakespeare

2997. It is not the stars to hold our destiny but in ourselves.
                                                    - William Shakespeare

2998. Give every man thy ear, but few thy voice.
                                                    - William Shakespeare

2999. Uneasy lies the head that wears a crown.
                                                    - William Shakespeare

3000. We succeeded in taking that picture *(shows a photograph of a black space with a tiny blue dot),* and, if you look at it, you see a dot. That's here. That's home. That's us. On it, everyone you ever heard of, every human being who ever lived, lived out their lives. The aggregate of all our joys and sufferings, thousands of confident religions, ideologies and economic doctrines, every hunter and forager, every hero and coward, every creator and destroyer of civilizations, every king and peasant, every young couple in love, every hopeful child, every mother and father, every inventor and explorer, every teacher of morals, every corrupt politician, every superstar, every supreme leader, every saint and sinner in the history of our species, lived there on a mote of dust, suspended in a sunbeam.

The earth is a very small stage in a vast cosmic arena. Think of the rivers of blood spilled by all those generals and emperors so that in glory and in triumph they could become the momentary masters of a fraction of a dot. Think of the endless cruelties visited by the inhabitants of one corner of the dot on scarcely distinguishable inhabitants of some other corner of the dot.

How frequent their misunderstandings, how eager they are to kill one another. Our posturing, our imagined self-importance, the delusion that we have some privileged position in the universe, are challenged by this point of light.

Our planet is a speck in the great enveloping cosmic dark. In our obscurity, there is no hint that help will come from elsewhere to save us from ourselves. It is up to us. It's been said that astronomy is a humbling, and I might add, a character-building experience. To my mind, there is perhaps no better demonstration of the folly of human conceits than this distant image of our tiny world.

To me, it underscores our responsibility to deal more kindly with one another and to preserve and cherish that pale blue dot, the only home we've ever known.

- Carl Sagan

www.ingramcontent.com/pod-product-compliance
Lightning Source LLC
Chambersburg PA
CBHW060451290526
45791CB00001B/71